BACKPACKER

THE OUTDOORS AT YOUR DOORSTEP

Leave No Trace

Second Edition

This little book should be required reading for every one of the ever-growing number of people looking for recreation in our finite wilderness. The author combines a sane approach to backcountry ethics with practical advice on topics like, well, using the bathroom in the woods.

—*Los Angeles Daily News,* Los Angeles

Wilderness ethics is a topic that deserves thoughtful consideration from time to time. A good jumping-off point is Leave No Trace.

—*Bend Bulletin,* Bend, OR

Learn how to enjoy a great camping spot and leave it in the same shape it was-or even better-with this new book.

—*Greeley Tribune,* Greeley, CO

This book is a must for anyone using the outdoors, even if you think you're familiar with LNT practices. I know you'll find something you haven't practiced in its 187 pages with plenty of pictures and illustrations.

—*Bangor Daily News,* Bangor, ME

Leave No Trace should be mandatory reading for all backpackers, campers, hunters, and hikers.

—*Idaho Statesman,* Boise, ID

One of the challenges of going into the wilderness is leaving no trace of your visit. This second edition book provides plenty of practical advice on how to do just that.

—*Deseret News,* Salt Lake City

BACKPACKER
THE OUTDOORS AT YOUR DOORSTEP

Leave No Trace

Second Edition

A GUIDE
TO THE NEW
WILDERNESS
ETIQUETTE

Annette McGivney

THE MOUNTAINEERS BOOKS

Published by
The Mountaineers Books
1001 SW Klickitat Way, Suite 201
Seattle, WA 98134

BACKPACKER
THE OUTDOORS AT YOUR DOORSTEP

33 East Minor Street
Emmaus, PA 18098

Published simultaneously in Great Britain by Cordee, 3a DeMontfort Street, Leicester, England, LE1 7HD.
Manufactured in the United States of America

Editor: Uma Kukathas
Copyeditors: Kris Fulsaas, Brenda Pittsley
Illustrator: Dawn Peterson
Cover and Book Design: The Mountaineers Books
Layout Artist: Jennifer LaRock Shontz

Cover photograph: *Eric Webb watching the sun set before staying at the Madison Hut (AMC Cabin) on the Airline Trail in the White Mountains.* © Rob Bossi
Frontispiece: *Backpacking in a remote section of popular Grand Canyon National Park* (Photo by Annette McGivney)

Library of Congress Cataloging-in-Publication Data

McGivney, Annette.
  Leave no trace : a guide to the new wilderness ethic / by Annette
McGivney.— 2nd ed.
     p. cm.
Includes bibliographical references and index.
  ISBN 0-89886-910-2 (pbk.)
  1. Outdoor recreation—Environmental aspects—United States. 2.
Low-impact camping—United States. I. Title.
  GV191.4.M35 2003
  796.54—dc21
                          2003007417

Contents

After a long, hot day backpacking to the bottom of the Grand Canyon, the author ▶ and a friend head for the cold waters of the Colorado River. *(Photo by Elias Butler)*

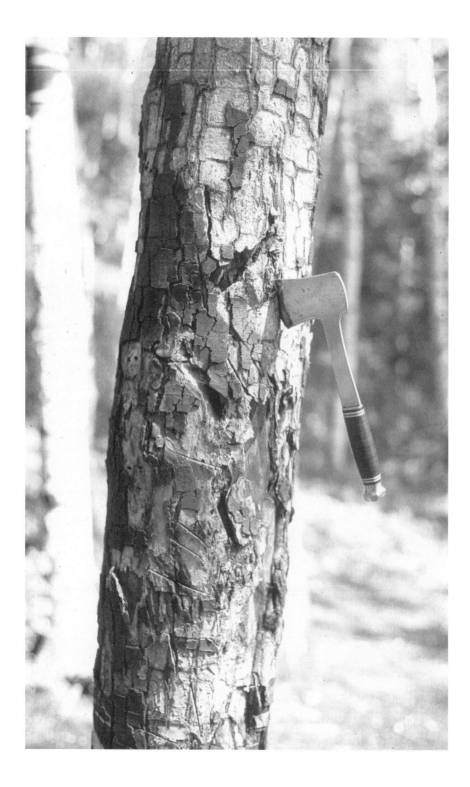

Preface

Imagine you have a houseguest who does not see anywhere in your house to hang his coat. So out come a hammer and a 4-inch nail, which he proceeds to drive into your oak paneling to create a makeshift coatrack. At dinner, your guest tosses food scraps on the carpet instead of saving them for the trash. And to top off the evening, this recipient of your hospitality relieves himself in the bathroom but carelessly discards used toilet paper on the floor instead of flushing it down the commode.

Such barbaric behavior sounds appalling, even unimaginable, in today's well-mannered society. You probably think you know no one who comes close to acting this way—that you would have to go back to the Middle Ages to find "civilized" adults tossing trash around in living areas and letting the nasties associated with bodily wastes fall where they may. But if you consider our nation's wilderness areas to be places as special and deserving of respect as a human home, then you probably know plenty of people who have behaved this way at one time or another—maybe even yourself.

In most places in the Lower 48 states, wilderness does not harbor human houses, but it is home to many creatures that deserve to live in an unpolluted environment. And for many of us humans—who over the last century have largely become urban animals—the wilderness is one of our favorite places to visit. Spending time in a natural environment, breathing clean air, drinking in wide-open spaces, witnessing the complex beauty of nature's handiwork is a joyous and much-needed experience for millions of Americans each year. And, considering how quickly urban development has spread in recent decades, and how little of the United States has been set aside as "forever protected" from development under the federal Wilderness Act of 1964, these precious few wild places are truly a privilege to visit and hardly the location for humans to despoil with their trash.

Yet, as recently as twenty-five years ago, it was common practice among upstanding American citizens to wreak havoc on the outdoor environment. Without

◀ The days of using a hatchet and other woodcraft tools are over. *(Photo by Jeff Marion)*

thinking twice, people set up camp in pristine areas and pounded pegs into trees to hang their lanterns and gear, left their trash in fire rings and makeshift garbage dumps, and encircled the area with human waste and the telltale "toilet-paper flowers." Youth groups perfected the art of camp craft by descending on an area en masse and going about digging latrines, constructing elaborate fire rings, chopping down trees for firewood and benches, cutting tree boughs for sleeping mats, and digging trenches around tents.

Thanks to a heightened environmental consciousness that blossomed over the last two decades, most outdoor enthusiasts are now much more aware of their impact on the land and no longer engage in the destructive "camp craft" practices of the days of yore. But beyond cleaning up your trash and not cutting down trees for firewood, how far should you go to minimize your impact? What is really important, from an environmental standpoint, and what is too extreme? Many environmentally conscious, recreation-minded people are unsure.

The purpose of this book is to answer these questions and introduce you to the principles of Leave No Trace (LNT), also known as the "new wilderness etiquette." This guide offers realistic LNT practices and techniques that can be applied to most outdoor pursuits.

To put it simply, Leave No Trace is the practice of traveling and camping with care when visiting wildlands. It requires deliberately planning and guiding outdoor experiences in order to not harm the environment or disturb others.

Leave No Trace is about helping people make sound environmental decisions when enjoying the great outdoors. Its aim is not ridding wildlands of all signs of human visitation. Unless people are barred from these areas completely, such an objective is impossible. The Leave No Trace ethic—as espoused by the Leave No Trace Center for Outdoor Ethics in Boulder, Colorado, as well as all federal land management agencies—supports the notion that humans belong in the wilderness; we just need to make our passing as undetectable as possible.

Attaining a balance between our desire to visit wildlands and doing what it takes to protect these sensitive places from too many visitors is a difficult and often conflicting goal. Land managers refer to this balance as the "limits of acceptable change." Leave No Trace brochures describe it as "minimizing impact." Either way, this new wilderness etiquette is a noble and necessary notion when you consider the growing human pressures on our public lands. LNT is the only way we can enjoy wilderness experiences without destroying the wilderness in the process.

As for how far you should go in adopting and practicing Leave No Trace techniques, it is up to you and what you are comfortable with (being environmentally responsible doesn't have to mean packing out human waste and drinking your dishwater). There are no LNT police out there enforcing a set of rules; motivation for abiding by this outdoor ethic should not come from guilt but a desire to respect and enjoy our limited wildlands. Traveling cleanly and quietly through the backcountry—leaving the land as you found it—is not only good for the environment but is often personally satisfying and leads to a heightened wilderness experience.

One final note about this book: the terms "wilderness," "backcountry," and "wildlands" are used synonymously throughout the text. Generally, all three terms are used to refer to public lands that are away from cities and are largely undeveloped. "Wilderness," however, specifically applies to land that is federally designated under the Wilderness Act of 1964. "Backcountry" and "wildlands" are more general terms that encompass wilderness areas, as well as all public lands that are mostly roadless and in a primitive condition.

Leave No Trace practices were originally aimed at protecting wilderness areas and educating backpackers and horsepackers visiting those places. However, the minimum-impact approach is now used to preserve the environmental integrity of all public lands, regardless of whether the land is formally protected under the Wilderness Act. Consequently, the Leave No Trace message—and this book—is aimed at all outdoor recreationists, from backpackers to mountain bikers to paddlers. I figure we could all benefit from a little schooling in wilderness etiquette to help us be better houseguests in the great outdoors.

Acknowledgments

Special thanks to David Cole of the U.S. Forest Service Aldo Leopold Research Institute and Jeff Marion of the National Park Service Cooperative Park Studies Unit at Virginia Polytechnic Institute and State University. Their generous help offering advice and supplying information was invaluable, and the principles of the Leave No Trace program are based upon their extensive research.

Also, heartfelt gratitude goes to Dana Watts at the Leave No Trace Center for Outdoor Ethics and to Pam Foti at Northern Arizona University's Parks and Recreation Management Program for their help and support in producing this second edition.

◀ Enjoying a protected wilderness in New Hampshire *(Photo by Robert Kozlow)*

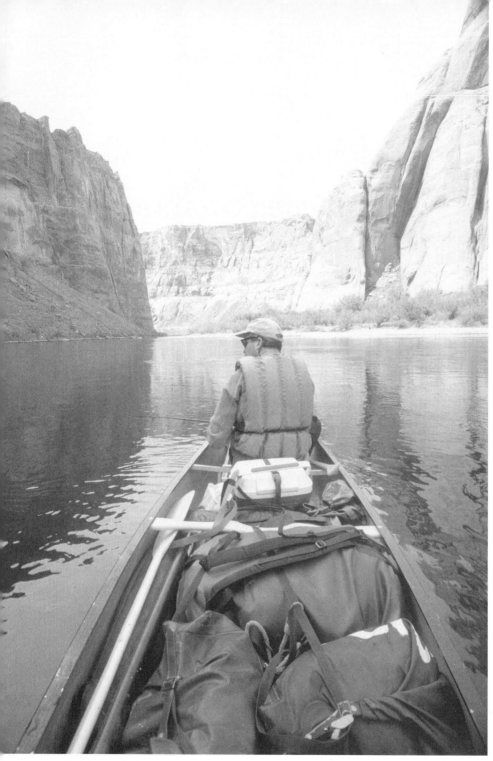

Paddling Lee's Ferry, Arizona *(Photo by Mike Frick)*

Introduction

America's Legacy of Wilderness and the Evolution of the Leave No Trace Ethic

Daniel Webster could not have been more misguided when in 1861 he shared his doubts about the push to fulfill the U.S. goal of Manifest Destiny and grow the nation all the way to the Pacific Ocean. As told in the book *Westward in Eden*, "What do we want of that vast and worthless area, that region of savages and wild beasts, of wind, of dust, of cactus and prairie dogs?" asked Webster of his fellow congressmen regarding the government's continued acquisition of western lands. "To what use could we ever hope to put those great deserts and those endless mountain ranges, impenetrable and covered to their base in eternal snow?"

Obviously, America's attitude toward its "untamed" public lands changed dramatically over the last 150 years. Pristine and rugged wilderness areas that were once considered worthless by prominent citizens like Daniel Webster are now cherished places guarded by the strictest of environmental laws. Unfortunately, the progression of the United States from a poor, young nation to a world superpower involved the development of billions of acres of pristine wildlands. And now that a consensus is emerging among U.S. citizens that our society needs wildlands, there is little true wilderness left to protect.

The current conservation ethic was preceded by a consumption ethic that emphasized using natural resources purely for economic gain. During most of the nineteenth century, U.S. public lands were valued not for recreation but for what could be extracted from them: gold, minerals, timber, rangeland, and an endless supply of acreage for homesteading.

A Public Lands Primer

Within the span of a century, the federally owned "public domain" has shrunk from more than a billion acres to some 730 million acres, or 32 percent of the total

Camping at the Grand Canyon *(Photo by Elias Butler)*

U.S. land area. What is left of our nation's federally owned lands is largely in Alaska and the western Lower 48 states, and most of it falls under the jurisdiction of four federal agencies: the U.S. Forest Service, the National Park Service, the U.S. Fish and Wildlife Service, and the Bureau of Land Management (BLM).

While each agency is managed to fulfill different mandates, all are charged with the dual responsibility of protecting our nation's natural resources and meeting the public's steadily expanding desire to recreate on federal lands. It is to this end that all four agencies have joined together in adopting and promoting the Leave No Trace ethic.

Although only a small percentage of federally owned lands is found east of the Mississippi, the eastern half of the United States nonetheless claims an abundance of recreational areas in the form of state-owned parks, preserves, forests, and game lands, as well as private preserves. In upstate New York, for example, Adirondack Park encompasses 2.5 million acres of public land, with 2000 miles of trails; Baxter State Park in Maine has 202,064 acres of wildlands with 175 miles of trails. Much of the 2100-mile Appalachian Trail, which extends from Maine to Georgia, goes through state lands and privately owned right-of-way.

Although public lands in the east are generally not as large as the vast expanses of western backcountry, they often have extensive trail networks and campgrounds, and suffer from the same risk of being loved to death as federally owned wildlands. Most of the state lands are managed by recreation-oriented agencies, such as the New York State Department of Environmental Conservation, which include staffs of rangers, biologists, and other professionals similar to those of the federal land management agencies. And, like the federal land management agencies, many of these state-run land management departments are actively involved in promoting the Leave No Trace program and teaching visitors about minimum-impact techniques.

How did we, as a nation, evolve from an anti-wilderness mentality like Daniel Webster's to the current state of affairs where government agencies promote the Leave No Trace ethic? The evolution of the conservation ethic and America's growing affinity for outdoor recreation really began to take shape with the landmark passage of the Wilderness Act in 1964.

A Return to the Wilderness

In an attempt to protect America's last vestiges of wildlands, and after years of debate, in 1964 Congress finally passed the sweeping measure that established the Wilderness Preservation System. The Wilderness Act incorporated 9.1 million acres of federal lands into the system. Today, designated wilderness totals more than 100 million acres and is found on lands managed by the Forest Service, Park Service, Fish and Wildlife Service, and BLM. These wilderness preserves, as defined by law, are "areas where the earth and its community of life are untrammeled by man, where man himself is a visitor who does not remain." The respective land management agency in charge of the land on which the designated areas are located is responsible for fulfilling the mandate of the Wilderness Act and keeping the preserves "untrammeled."

Consequently, motorized vehicles and mountain bikes are banned from all federal wilderness areas. The construction of roads and any kind of commercial development is not allowed. Unless it was "grandfathered" in when a specific wilderness area was designated by Congress, consumptive uses such as grazing, mining, logging, and oil extraction are also off-limits. The only way to travel through a wilderness area is self-propelled by foot, pack animal, or paddle.

After the Wilderness Act was passed, the various federal land management agencies conducted inventories of their holdings and identified all roadless areas larger than 5000 acres considered suitable for wilderness designation. In most states, the wilderness designation process has been completed and Congress has passed state wilderness bills that supposedly set aside our nation's major roadless areas for preservation. Although obtaining wilderness status for the 107 million acres that are currently part of the Wilderness Preservation System is an environmental victory, the battle for preservation of wildlands is far from over.

One need only leaf through *The Big Outside: A Descriptive Inventory of the Big Wilderness Areas of the United States*, by Dave Foreman and Howie Wolke, to get a feel for all the worthy wildlands that are not designated as wilderness and given the protection they deserve. Even though the opening paragraph of the Wilderness Act clearly states "it is the policy of Congress to secure for the American people of present and future generations the benefits of an enduring resource of wilderness," when it comes to politics, short-term gains almost always win over long-term goals. In western states, where most of the eligible, large roadless areas are located, large chunks of federal lands that conservationists say should be a shoo-in for wilderness designation have been passed over because of objections from consumptive users of the land such as logging and mining companies.

In Arizona, for example, the Forest Service identified 2.1 million acres as suitable for wilderness designation, and conservation groups argued that all of the land should be protected under the Wilderness Preservation System. But, in the end, only 767,000 acres were federally designated under the 1984 Arizona Wilderness Act, and the largest stands of old-growth ponderosa pine forest in the Southwest were left open to logging. Elsewhere in the west, wars over wilderness designation still rage in Utah where conservationists are pushing to protect 9 million acres, but the state's congressional delegation wants one-third of that amount.

Meanwhile, federal land managers are struggling in many designated wilderness areas to keep the land in an "untrammeled" condition. As David Cole of the U.S. Forest Service's Aldo Leopold Research Institute observes in a report titled *Wilderness Recreation Use Trends*, "Recreation use of the National Wilderness Preservation

System increased almost sixfold between 1965 and 1994 when recreation use approached 17 million visitor days." (A visitor day is defined as one person visiting the area for twelve hours.) Cole adds, "People are recreating in designated wilderness more than ever." He states that in 1994, the year he conducted the study, "recreation use intensity, excluding Alaska, was as high as it has ever been."

Cole further notes that, compared to their backpacking brethren of the 1970s, wilderness travelers of the twenty-first century like to wander off the beaten path in search of adventure. "There's a cultural shift to push the envelope and go off designated trails," he said. "Back in the 1970s, once you were away from the trail you saw very little sign of humans. Now I'm seeing far more trampling and other disturbance impacts off trails. People like to pioneer their own routes."

While backpacking and horsepacking in wilderness areas continue to have a steady, if slightly increased, participation rate, it is the day hiker who seems to be headed to these preserves in droves. According to the most recent Outdoor Recreation Participation Trends report produced by the U.S. Forest Service, 48 million people—24 percent of the U.S. population age sixteen years and older—say they go day hiking. It is by far the fastest-growing activity in wilderness areas. Not surprisingly, wildlands located within a few hours' drive of metropolitan areas are most heavily distressed by increased visitation.

In fact, George Nickas, executive director of the Missoula, Montana–based environmental group Wilderness Watch believes recreation is the number one threat to wilderness. "Now, just plain old hiking and camping are a problem because there are so many of us doing it," he noted. Individually, each hiker is relatively benign. But, collectively, we have a huge impact.

Leave No Trace Is Born

Dealing with increasing visitation and the resulting environmental impact is part and parcel of being a land manager today, but few managers were prepared thirty years ago for the recreation boom that happened after the Wilderness Act was passed. A public survey conducted by Edward Spencer and others in 1965 for the Bureau of Outdoor Recreation showed that 9.9 million Americans hiked or backpacked. This figure increased to more than 28 million when the survey was repeated in 1977.

The problem back then was not only with the number of people descending upon wilderness areas, but also with the high-impact approach most people took (albeit unknowingly) when visiting the great outdoors. Millions of people visiting the backcountry and practicing camping techniques from a bygone era caused wildlands in many places to look more like the back alleys of third-world villages rather than land that had been set aside for the express purpose of protection from development.

Alpine lakes became polluted from human waste; trails eroded to levels that were sometimes knee-deep; campsites became devoid of vegetation and were often host to growing mounds of discarded refuse, including everything from tin cans to broken backpacks. It all added up to a big dilemma for the land managers who are charged with dual responsibilities of environmental protection of the resource and accommodation of the public's desire to recreate on public lands.

"In the 1970s, it was socially acceptable to have fire rings and litter everywhere at wilderness campsites," recalls Tom Alt, a forestry technician with the Beartooth District of the Custer National Forest in Montana and Wyoming. In fact, land managers in the Beartooth–Absaroka Wilderness during that time found themselves packing out "mule-trains" of trash left behind by careless campers.

To get a handle on overuse and abuse of America's wilderness areas, land managers had two primary options—they could close damaged areas to the public or, as Alt explains, they could try to educate wilderness users in more environmentally sound camping techniques, to "show people a better way." The educational program that Alt and his Forest Service colleagues developed sixteen years ago came to be called "No Trace." Meanwhile, the Forest Service in Utah had developed a similar program called "Leave No Trace" to deal with visitor impact in the Uinta Mountains.

"When [No Trace] first got started, we had to teach people the basics—that you did not leave garbage piles, that you did not tie horses to trees, and that you did not need to have large campfires," says Alt. "People generally knew littering was wrong, but they were not aware of the impact of human waste in the wilderness, and how long it takes toilet paper to decompose." Alt's district, along with other National Forest districts across the country, also began implementing policies dictating how far camps should be set back from water, campfire restrictions, and visitor permit systems. "People have generally been very receptive to the low-impact message, but, for some, old ways die hard," he says.

Nevertheless, Alt's education program has had a big impact, reaching some 55,000 people in Montana, including many schoolchildren and outdoor groups. Well-meaning visitors are no longer leaving trash piles, cutting tree boughs, or trenching around tents in the Beartooth–Absaroka Wilderness. "I say this with trepidation, but things have gotten better," notes Alt. "We have more visitors now than in the '70s, but the impacts are less."

The LNT Message Spreads

The success of Alt's program in the Beartooths encouraged other land managers across the country to embrace the concept of a public education program to teach people techniques in minimum-impact camping and wilderness travel. While closure of overused areas, visitor quota systems, and implementation of designated campsites have served as important management tools over the last few decades for keeping our precious wildlands from being loved to death, visitor education is by far the most socially palatable and often the most effective solution.

By the early 1980s there were numerous minimum-impact education programs circulating through the federal land management agencies. Slogans such as "pack it in; pack it out," "tread lightly," "take only pictures, leave only footprints," and "give a hoot, don't pollute" became familiar to backcountry visitors. Just about everyone got the message that litter was a big no-no, that human fecal matter required a proper burial, and that toilet paper was not to be treated as some kind of ground cover. Beyond these basic dos and don'ts, however, the low-impact mantra varied greatly with each program, each land management agency, and almost every district office. The lack of a uniform message led to confusion among wilderness users and, in many cases, made the land manager's dual job of recreation enabler and environmental steward that much more difficult.

Enter Bill Thompson, a thirty-eight-year U.S. Forest Service veteran who has worked in Forest Service districts throughout the west. In 1990, the Forest Service asked Thompson if he would be the agency's first Leave No Trace coordinator and promote the minimum-impact concept as a national program. By 1993 a "memorandum of understanding" was signed between the four federal land management agencies (U.S. Forest Service, National Park Service, Bureau of Land Management, and U.S. Fish and Wildlife Service) and the nonprofit National Outdoor Leadership School (NOLS), which established Leave No Trace as the nation's official wilderness ethics program. (Founded in 1965 and based in Lander, Wyoming, NOLS is a wilderness-based, nonprofit school focusing on teaching leadership and outdoor skills.)

Thompson enlisted NOLS to spearhead the education component of the program. NOLS collaborated with the BLM, Forest Service, National Park Service, and recreation ecologists Jeff Marion and David Cole to develop the basic principles of the Leave No Trace program and a standard LNT curriculum. NOLS staff members Drew Leemon, Susan Chadwick Brame, and John Gookin drew from information on minimum-impact research and techniques they had developed for NOLS instructors to create LNT materials that could be mass-marketed across the country. Perhaps most significantly, the NOLS team designed the five-day Master Educator course for land managers, outfitters, youth group leaders, and others. At last, there was one cohesive, consistent message going out to wildland users.

In 1994, Leave No Trace, Inc. was created to expand the scope and reach of the program. Based in Boulder, Colorado, the nonprofit agency was charged with coordinating all national LNT partnership, licensing, and fund-raising efforts. Under the leadership of executive director Dana Watts, the organization sought to unite the four federal land management agencies with manufacturers and retailers of outdoor gear, user groups, and educators who were involved in spreading the

LNT message. The fledgling organization grew quickly as did the popularity of the Leave No Trace program.

In 2002, LNT Inc. changed its name to the Leave No Trace Center for Outdoor Ethics to better reflect the organization's broadened scope, including overseeing all public outreach, education, and fundraising for the Leave No Trace program. The center has seventeen staff members and a budget of more than 1.2 million dollars. Working in partnership with the Leave No Trace Center, five Master Educator course providers teach the Master Educator courses at outdoor locations across the United States—NOLS, the Appalachian Mountain Club (AMC), Landmark Learning, the Wilderness Education Association, and the U. S. Forest Service Ninemile Wildlands Training Center. There are now three international branches—Leave No Trace/Sans Trace Canada, Leave No Trace Australia, and Leave No Trace Ireland. In addition, they have an active kids education program that was created in partnership with REI called the PEAK Program (Promoting Environmental Awareness in Kids). To date 100,000 kids have been through the PEAK program.

According to Watts, there are now more than 2,500 "Masters" who've completed the program's capstone course. Even more have been reached by the Leave No Trace Center's "Traveling Trainer" program, co-sponsored by Subaru of America. For more than five years, two couples ("Team East" and "Team West") have driven around the country, stopping at hundreds of outdoor retailers, national parks, and other public lands to spread the Leave No Trace message. Watts estimates the program has trained more than 90,000 individuals in the Leave No Trace ethic. (For information on Leave No Trace education courses, materials, and membership, see the appendix.)

The Leave No Trace Center recently began research to evaluate the effectiveness of the outdoor ethics program. In 2002, the organization completed its first Leave No Trace laboratory project where recreationists in Colorado's San Juan Mountains were monitored for their receptivity to the LNT message. "We found there are some things we need to work on," says Watts. "But, overall, we learned that our message is effective and can actually change some user behavior."

Greg Hansen already knew this. Currently the national Leave No Trace program coordinator for the U.S. Forest Service, Hansen has been monitoring recreation impacts in Arizona's Tonto National Forest Superstition Wilderness for fifteen years. The wilderness borders the Phoenix metropolitan area and receives heavy use. "After just five years of aggressive education and working the LNT message into everything we do, we've been able to measure significant on-the-ground improvements in the wilderness," Hansen reports. He attributes the education efforts to a 100-percent reduction in litter, a 65-percent reduction in fire rings, and a 90-percent reduction in trampling impacts.

Sunset in Sedona, Arizona *(Photo by Elias Butler)* ▶

How the West Was Lost and Won

A History of the U.S. Frontier and Federal Land Management

Beginning with the Louisiana Purchase in 1803, in which the United States doubled its geographic size with the stroke of a pen, the vast wilderness between the Mississippi River and the Pacific Ocean became American territory. Treaties and purchases between the U.S. government and Spain, Great Britain, Mexico, and the Republic of Texas grew our nation from sea to shining sea in just fifty years. Plus, the acquisition of Alaska from Russia in 1867 added another 365 million acres to the U.S. land base.

While the United States was acquiring some of the most scenic and ecologically diverse wilderness on the planet, the federal government's plan was not to preserve it for posterity but, rather, to use the land to grow the nation's economy. In 1812, the General Land Office was established to "dispose" of federally owned lands—called the "public domain"—and put the abundant natural resources in the hands of private individuals and enterprises for development. Because much of the land in the East and Midwest had already passed into private ownership by then, most of the public domain that was up for grabs was in the West—the rugged Rockies, the grasslands of the Great Plains, the canyons of the Southwest, and the towering redwood forests of the Pacific Coast.

Although the idea of wholesale development of these pristine lands for the sake of commerce makes modern-day conservationists cringe, few questioned the motives or methods for profiting from western wilderness in the nineteenth century. In fact, as William K. Wayant points out in *Westward in Eden*, destroying the wilderness was cause for great excitement and hype among many business-minded people, such as Thaddeus Mason Harris of Massachusetts. In *Westward in Eden*, we find Harris's account of the pioneer settlements he saw on his journey down the Ohio River through the Northwest Territory in 1803:

"When we see the land cleared of those enormous trees with which it was overgrown, and the cliffs and quarries converted into materials for building, we cannot help dwelling upon the industry and art of man, which by dint of toil and perseverance can change the desert into a fruitful field, and shape the rough rock to use. . . . When the solitary waste is peopled, and convenient habitations arise amidst the former retreats of wild beasts; when the silence of nature is succeeded by the buzz of employment . . . when we behold competence and plenty springing from the bosom of dreary forests—what a lesson is afforded of the benevolent intentions of Providence!"

The Homestead Act of 1862 was the most benevolent in a series of federal laws that encouraged unrestricted settlement of the West in an attempt to fulfill such "providence." Under the measure, any hearty soul could claim 160 acres of public domain as his private property just by living on it for five years. It was an enticing offer for millions of people residing east of the Mississippi, as well as European immigrants fresh off the boat from land-scarce countries. But as Roderick Nash points out in his book *Wilderness and the American Mind*, homesteading rugged western lands was no panacea; consequently, the wilderness was viewed by frontier settlers as Public Enemy Number One—right up there with the devil.

"Two components figured in the American pioneer's bias against wilderness," writes Nash. "On the direct, physical level, it constituted a formidable threat to his very survival. Safety and comfort, even necessities like food and shelter, depended on overcoming the wild environment. In addition, civilized man faced the danger of succumbing to the wilderness of his surroundings and reverting to savagery himself. The pioneer, in short, lived too close to wilderness for appreciation."

In the end, much of the American wilderness was conquered and between 1781 and 1976 the federal government disposed of more than 1.1 billion acres of public domain. Of this amount, only 287 million acres went to individual settlers under the Homestead Act. While much of the West proved to be too rugged for settlement by individuals schooled in East Coast farming techniques, the resource-rich land became a plunder playground for private enterprise. The General Land Office was corrupt throughout its ranks and routinely made shady deals with railroad companies and land speculators; illegal logging and mining were rampant on public lands, and some of America's greatest scenic wonders including Yellowstone, Yosemite, and the Grand Canyon were gravely threatened by private development.

Although many pioneers and/or profiteers were continuing the quest to conquer western wilderness, an ethic of conservation was beginning to take shape in the United States during the mid- to late 1800s. In 1872, Yellowstone became the first national park in the world. In 1890, Yosemite, Sequoia, and General Grant (now part of Sequoia) were also established as national parks. The following year, Congress passed the Forest Reserve Act, which gave the president authority to claim an unlimited amount of public domain as essentially off-limits to unrestricted logging, and put control of the nation's timber and water resources back in the hands of the federal government. The Antiquities Act of 1906, created largely in response to the pillaging of prehistoric Native American archaeological sites in the Southwest, allowed for the establishment of national monuments on any federal land that the president deemed to be of "scientific, historic, or scenic value." Within ten years, twenty national monuments had been declared, including the Grand Canyon.

By 1900, the western frontier was essentially closed and a series of laws and agencies had been established to guard against the kinds of abuses of the public domain that had characterized the previous century. Federal programs were established to allow private interests to profit from the natural resources of the public domain. Grazing, mining, and logging on federal lands was (and still is) common practice, and it became the economic foundation of many western states.

Chapter 1

Principles to Live By
SEVEN THINGS YOU CAN DO TO KEEP THE WILD IN WILDERNESS

Just as our nation's founding fathers agonized over the Articles of Confederation in the U.S. Constitution, Leave No Trace board members spent weeks debating the program's unifying principles around which the program revolves. Everything from the exact wording to the philosophy of the program was deliberated by a group of land managers, recreation ecologists, and outdoor educators charged with defining the principles of a national Leave No Trace program.

Over the last decade the principles were modified twice in an effort to make the minimum impact message as cohesive and effective as possible. The end result is the Seven Principles of Leave No Trace. According to program executive director Dana Watts, the "goal is to build a critical mass of educated users who will make the seven principles the standard code of conduct on public lands." These principles are the foundation of what has become a wilderness etiquette, an ethic toward recreating in the backcountry that is eons from the days when it was common practice to turn campsites into garbage dumps.

But don't confuse the Seven Principles with the Ten Commandments. When teaching LNT skills and ethics, NOLS stresses that the basic principles around which the minimum-impact ethic is built are not hard-and-fast rules, but guidelines

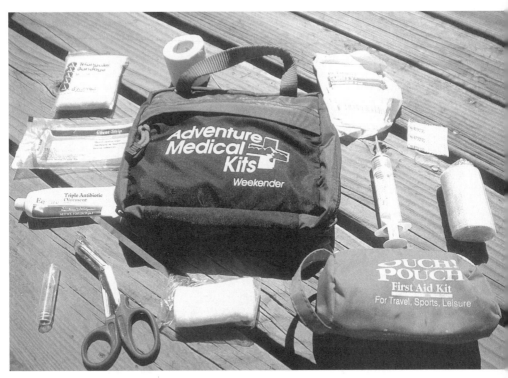

Be prepared. *(Photo by Annette McGivney)*

aimed at helping backcountry users make ecologically sound decisions in various environments and situations. Michael Cheek, NOLS Leave No Trace program coordinator, also emphasizes that "the principles are based on scientific research rather than arbitrary rules. To date there is not a significant amount of research available, but the long-term goal of the national Leave No Trace program is to maintain a science foundation as the basis for LNT practices."

The principles of Leave No Trace are expanded upon throughout this book, but here is the encapsulated version of seven guidelines to live by when visiting the great outdoors:

Plan ahead and prepare.

- ▲ Call ahead to the place you intend to visit to find out about any special environmental concerns, regulations, or permits.
- ▲ Be prepared for harsh conditions by bringing proper equipment and knowing how to use it.
- ▲ Carry and know how to use a map and compass.
- ▲ Carefully plan meals so that there is no food waste. Reduce your amount of trash by repackaging food in reusable containers.

- Invest in modern gear that aids in both safe and environmentally responsible camping. Use a lightweight stove to replace the need for cooking over fires; get a tent with a watertight floor; become the proud owner of a trowel to aid in the digging of cat holes.
- Try to stay away from popular areas during times of high use, such as holidays and weekends. If you are in a group of four or more, take special care to avoid popular areas during busy times.

Camp and travel on durable surfaces.

- Help mitigate trampling and erosion problems by staying on designated trails. Walk in single file in the middle of the path.
- Don't shortcut trails.
- When traveling cross-country where there are no trails, try to stay on the most durable surfaces—rock, gravel, dry grasses, or snow.
- In areas frequented by visitors, camp at a designated site that shows obvious signs of use—soil is compacted, vegetation is sparse. Keep your activities concentrated in the affected area.
- If you are lucky enough to be in a pristine area that shows little or no sign of human visitation, disperse your individual impact by camping in a never-before-used site. Move your campsite daily in pristine locations to avoid leaving an impression. Stay away from campsites that have already been lightly marked.
- Protect sensitive riparian areas and lakeshores by camping at least 200 feet from lakes and streams.

Dispose of waste properly.

- Basically, if you packed it in, you need to pack it out.
- Keep your gear organized in camp so that you do not accidentally leave something behind.
- Burying trash is not a good idea because wildlife will just dig it up, and burning it is not environmentally sound either. Carry a plastic bag to pack your trash (and perhaps that of others).
- Practice good sanitation. Use established facilities (flush, vault, or pit toilets) whenever they're available.
- Where there are no facilities, bury human waste in a cat hole that is 4 to 8 inches deep and at least 200 feet from water, camp, or trails.
- Scrutinize your need for toilet paper; nature provides a variety of environmentally friendly tissue alternatives. If you prefer to use toilet paper, pack it out.
- To wash yourself or your dishes, carry water 200 feet from streams or lakes, and use small amounts of biodegradable soap. Strain dishwater with a cloth and then scatter the water or sump.

Leave what you find (Ancestral Puebloan petroglyph, southern Utah). *(Photo by Mike Frick)*

Leave what you find.

- For starters, it is against federal law to disturb archaeological or historic sites. Do not disturb these relics of our nation's heritage, and camp well away from such sites.

- Avoid altering a campsite—such as driving a nail into a tree or making a bench out of a log—to accommodate your desire for comfort. If you move a log or rock to improve a sleeping area, replace it when leaving camp.

- Many recreationists unknowingly introduce invasive plant species. Before each trip, clean your gear and boots to get rid of tiny plant seeds that could hitch-hike into the wilderness.

- Take home memories instead of souvenirs such as interesting rocks, seashells, or wildflowers.

- Give children a camera and encourage them to document their experience with photos rather than by collecting items or disturbing the landscape.

Minimize campfire impacts.

▲ Although a cozy tradition, campfires can permanently scar an area. Use a stove instead.

▲ Use a headlamp and/or candle lantern for light at the campsite.

▲ If you must have a fire, use an existing fire ring or build a no-trace mound or pan fire.

▲ For fuel, gather sticks on the ground that are no larger in diameter than an adult's wrist. Do not pull branches off dead or downed trees.

▲ When vacating a site, put out your fire completely, pack out all unburned trash from the fire ring, and scatter the cool ashes over a large area well away from camp.

Respect wildlife.

▲ Observe wildlife from a distance. A simple rule of thumb is that if the animal moves in response to your presence, you are too close.

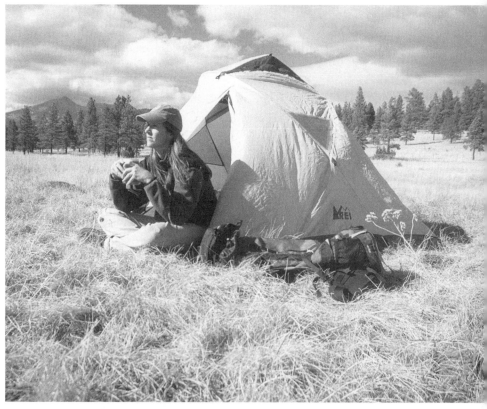

Camp on durable surfaces. *(Photo by Annette McGivney)*

- The wilderness is not a zoo. Never feed the animals, even if they beg for handouts.
- Take care not to drop food scraps around camp that will attract animals. Even seemingly harmless trash items like an apple core or an orange peel can disrupt their natural diet.
- Protect wildlife and your food by storing food and trash securely. Hang your food in bear country.
- Wildlife is especially vulnerable during spring mating and nesting seasons and during winter when they are conserving precious calories. Be especially vigilant during these times to avoid disturbing animals.
- Even if your dog is well trained there's a good chance instinct will prevail and it will harass wildlife. If you choose to take your pet on wilderness trips, keep it leashed on the trail and under control in camp.

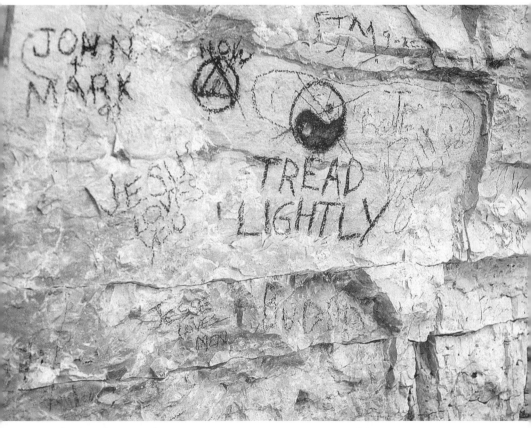

Graffiti in Sycamore Canyon Wilderness Area, Arizona *(Photo by Mike Frick)*

Be considerate of other visitors.

▲ Do what you can to protect the wilderness resource of solitude.

▲ Minimize noise. Let nature's sounds prevail. Wear headphones if you prefer to listen to music.

▲ Keep a low profile. Take rest breaks on durable surfaces out of sight from the trail. When possible, pitch your tent so that it's not visible to campers nearby.

▲ Yield to other visitors. This fosters goodwill and prevents trail widening. When you encounter pack stock, step downhill from the trail to allow the party to pass.

Although the Leave No Trace concept can be boiled down to a few basic guidelines, it actually goes far beyond convincing people to pack out what they pack in. It is about gaining an understanding of the environment and knowing how to enjoy America's precious wildlands without harming them. And it is about having respect for fellow recreationists and their desire to enjoy the land. Protecting the backcountry through wilderness designations and land management regulations is not enough. Ultimately, preservation of our nation's wildlands comes down to visitor attitudes and our willingness to practice this new wilderness etiquette.

Chapter 2

All About Camping
LNT GUIDELINES FOR FINDING A SITE,
CLEAN CAMPFIRES, AND KITCHEN DUTY

We stood around the clearing like eager medical students listening to our physician-professor course through the processes of deductive reasoning. A questionable campsite in Wyoming's Wind River Range was our test patient, and we were to diagnose its condition and, ultimately, determine whether the site should exist at all.

"It obviously has been frequently used for a long time. And it is unofficial (not a designated site of the national forest)," observed Rich Brame, a NOLS staff member and our teacher for the 1996 LNT Master Educator Course. We students took these factors under advisement as we examined the campsite in question for telling environmental and sociological symptoms. A big fire ring in the middle was fortified with large, blackened rocks; a pile of branches and twigs next to the ring waited for the next group of campers; several logs were placed around the fire ring as benches; the lower reaches of a few trees appeared to have been stripped for wood; and, compared to the surrounding forest, the ground was largely devoid of leaves, duff, and new plant life. We paced the perimeter of the site to complete our examination. Several well-worn trails ventured into surrounding thickets . . . potty paths. The size of the site appeared to be growing over time as people sought out new boulders and trees on which to prop packs and place equipment, and there was a smaller, secondary fire ring off to the side.

We discussed the general condition of the patient. On a scale of one to five, with five being the worst, the environmental health of the campsite was (in medical lingo) a "Code 4." But the good news was that the poor condition was stabilized and there was not much else that could happen to make the site any worse. The location was not a problem; it was at least 200 feet away from a nearby lake and well off the main trail. "A lot of people have been coming here," said Brame. "If this site were to be closed, they would just camp somewhere else nearby and damage that location."

We concluded, with the help of Brame's guidance, that although the site is not "official" it has been established through historic use and should continue to exist in an effort to keep recreational activities in the area concentrated. We (as concerned citizens and dedicated LNT practitioners) decided to administer the following treatment: scatter the pile of wood and dismantle the log benches to discourage large fires; pack out any trash that may make the site less appealing to prospective campers; and dismantle the secondary fire ring.

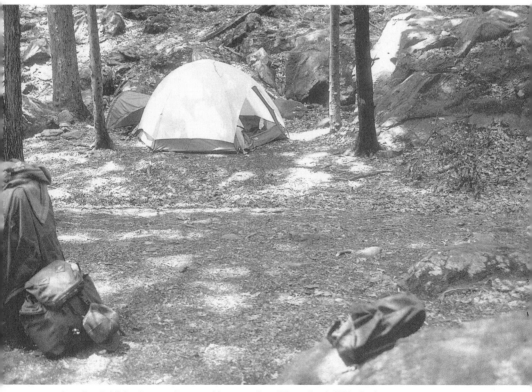

A well-established campsite, good for camping *(Photo by Jeff Marion)*

Such is the complex process of Leave No Trace camping. Like a doctor diagnosing a patient, often there are no clear-cut answers, so campers must use their best judgment in deciding, for instance, where to park their tent for the night. Armed with knowledge of the environment and an understanding of minimum-impact guidelines, the consummate LNT camper relies on reason rather than rules to make the proper choices—from deciding whether to have a fire to determining the most durable spot for the camp "kitchen."

The Perfect LNT Campsite

If you are truly interested in protecting the environmental health of an area, keep in mind that the proverbial "perfect campsite" is more than a level spot with a beautiful view and water nearby. Because the activity of camping is responsible for the majority of recreational damage to our wildlands, where you choose to spend the night is likely the most important environmental decision you will make on a trip.

Falling under the LNT principle of "camp and travel on durable surfaces," three general campsite guidelines are espoused by minimum-impact experts:

▲ When in a popular area, camp on a well-worn site to concentrate use.

▲ When in a rarely visited, pristine area, disperse impact by camping in a spot that has never been used before.

▲ Avoid sites where signs of use are moderately to barely visible. This will give the land a chance to heal.

▲ No matter where you are, you can reduce trampling to the site by wearing lightweight shoes, such as sport sandals, when in camp.

Always keep in mind an LNT truism from John Hart, author of *Walking Softly in the Wilderness:* "The perfect campsite is found, not made." This means that, no matter where you decide to bed down, you should never rearrange the landscape to suit your needs—please don't dig up plants and rocks (little critters live under there) to create a tent pad, or move logs and boulders to use as camp furniture.

Choosing a Site in Popular Areas

According to Forest Service research biologist David Cole, the biggest environmental problem in wilderness areas over the past two decades is not the deterioration of popular, longtime campsites but the proliferation of new sites. Back in the 1970s, popular campsites such as horsepacker camps in Montana and Idaho's River of No Return Wilderness or shelters along the Appalachian Trail in North Carolina and Virginia looked like shantytowns. Through visitor education and various land management policies—primarily restricting group size—these wilderness slums have largely disappeared, but environmental degradation caused by campers continues.

The Case for Designated Campsites

Back in the 1970s when recreational use of our nation's wildlands was skyrocketing, land managers began researching and monitoring the environmental condition of camp- sites. They found in many popular areas across the country that it was not just the most heavily used campsites that were being turned into ecological wastelands; sites receiv- ing only moderate use (about thirty nights per year) were also going downhill fast. For example, in Minnesota's Boundary Waters Canoe Area, the damage to most campsites went well beyond a proliferation of fire rings and soil trampling. Repeated exposure to human visitation, especially by large groups, was permanently altering the ecological communities of these areas—the rich topsoil had disappeared, leaving only nutrient- poor mineral soil; native understory plants could not survive and exotic species were taking over; mature trees were dying and young saplings did not stand a chance.

Land managers across the country—from Virginia's Shenandoah National Park to the Grand Canyon to Oregon's Eagle Cap Wilderness—adopted various strategies to deal with the problem. One of the most seemingly logical courses of action was to temporarily close overused campsites and ask visitors to pitch their tents elsewhere until the damaged areas healed. However, it soon became obvious that it takes far longer for the land to regenerate than it does for it to deteriorate. So the end result of temporary campsite closures in most cases was that a larger portion of the land was disturbed than if nothing had been done at all. Such were the findings of David Cole in "Monitoring the Conditions of Wilderness Campsites," a 1983 study of temporary camp- site closures at Big Lake Creek in Montana's Selway–Bitterroot Wilderness.

In 1973, approximately fifteen well-defined and environmentally damaged camp- sites had developed around the shore of the popular Big Lake Creek. Land managers closed seven of the sites and posted signs directing campers to alternative sites a short distance from the lake. But after eight years, vegetation recovery on the closed sites was minimal and campers had created seven new sites next to the closed areas. "The pro- gram to restore overused sites can hardly be judged a success," said the study. "In fact it was counterproductive. The major effect of the program was to increase the total area disturbed by camping by about 50 percent."

Another faulty land management approach frequently implemented by the Forest Service during the '70s and '80s was, according to Cole, relying on "dilution as the solution." Attempting to mitigate environmental impacts by encouraging campers to spread out and avoid heavily used sites was generally ineffective and just created a bigger ecological mess. Offering an analogy to the campsite dilution solution, Cole said, "We could spread our trash across the entire planet rather than concentrating it in landfills, and it would decompose faster. But more land would be impacted. And who wants to look at trash everywhere? I think we all prefer landfills."

As a result of research from Cole and others, the general consensus among land managers today is that containment is usually the best approach to managing campsite impact. In popular wilderness areas and national parks, this is typically accomplished through permit systems in which visitors are required to camp at designated sites or zones, and/or numbers of visitors are limited by site availability. More than a quarter of our national parks now allow backcountry camping only at designated sites. And some of the most visited destinations, including Grand Canyon, Glacier, Yellowstone, Rocky

Today's wilderness travelers, it seems, always look for a better campsite. Even when there is a selection of suitable, established places to pitch their tent, campers "pioneer" a new site near existing ones because it is a little cleaner or more private or has a better view. "For example, in two drainages in the Eagle Cap Wilderness," said Cole in his report "Campsites in Three Western Wildernesses" on the proliferation problem, "the number of campsites increased from 336 in 1975 to 748 in 1990."

This trend, if compared to the complexion of a typical adolescent, is like giving a wildland area a face full of acne and pockmarks instead of just one or two large blemishes. On an individual basis, a big bull's-eye zit may seem more traumatic, but it is the many blemishes of widespread acne that, though individually smaller, lead to an overall unsightly appearance and scar the skin. So it is with camping—a lot of little, seemingly innocuous sites are far more damaging to the environmental health of an area than a few well-used sites.

Consequently, it is the responsibility of every Leave No Trace practitioner to sacrifice a little in the way of personal aesthetics in the interest of environmental preservation by camping in well-used sites whenever possible. With the exception of perhaps a few remote roadless areas in the West, most public lands in the Lower 48 that have trails also have an adequate supply of established campsites. You will be rewarded in minimum-impact heaven if you bite the bullet and go ahead and camp at a site that is somewhat trampled, perhaps with a few beer cans in the fire ring and toilet paper flowers in the bushes, rather than bedding down at a relatively undisturbed but more scenic site nearby. Do you want to be responsible for giving the land another zit?

Such an ethic is working wonders to improve the backcountry complexion of Shenandoah National Park in Virginia. Five years ago, USGS research biologist Jeff

An overused campsite. Stay off. *(Photo by Jeff Marion)*

Marion embarked on a project to reduce the proliferation of campsites in heavily used areas of the park. "In one drainage, for example, we located about fifty campsites but only ten of the sites were being used on a high-use weekend," said Marion. So Marion and his crew picked the twenty most environmentally resistant sites and

Moderately impacted campsite

Heavily impacted campsite

closed the rest. Backcountry visitors are now educated about the need to camp only in "established sites." So far, there are plenty of campsites for all and Marion reports the closed sites are "recovering nicely." In this case, a containment strategy coupled with visitor education is working as well as other, less popular management tools such as quotas systems. "The total area of disturbance has been reduced substantially," says Marion. "And the remaining open sites have not significantly deteriorated from the increased use."

The perfect Leave No Trace campsite should be located well out of view from the main trail and at least 200 feet from water sources. The best surfaces for camping are slickrock or rock outcroppings, gravel bars, and sandy beaches because they are so resistant to human corrosion. Other surfaces found to be highly resilient to camper trampling are dry, grassy meadows and open forests with a grassy understory. Environments that are least resistant to human impact are dense forests with a heavily vegetated understory of broad-leafed and woody plants.

Try to find an existing, visibly damaged site in one of these more resilient environments. Such a site is likely to have a fire ring, and ground vegetation will be worn away over most of the area, although decomposing leaves and needles may be present in spots. Stay off sites where prior use is barely noticeable, or where use has been so severe that the soil is eroded, the ground is completely barren, and tree roots are exposed.

LNT Basics: Choosing a Campsite

Use these guidelines to choose a campsite, but more than anything, rely on your own good judgment.

▲ The perfect Leave No Trace campsite should be located well out of view from the main trail and at least 200 feet (about 75 paces) from water sources.

▲ The campsite surfaces found most resistant to human corrosion are slickrock or rock outcroppings; gravel bars and sandy beaches; dry, grassy meadows; and open forests with a grassy understory.

In Popular Areas

Whenever possible, park your tent at an established campsite where impact from previous campers is clearly visible.

▲ Established campsites typically contain a fire ring and the ground shows signs of trampling from people and/or pack stock.

▲ If a site is so heavily used that the ground is barren and eroded, and tree roots are exposed, camp elsewhere so the land can heal.

In Pristine Areas

In pristine areas where no established campsites are available, camp at a spot that appears to never have been used rather than in an area that shows modest signs of human disturbance.

▲ Make your camp on a highly durable or resilient surface, such as slickrock, gravel, or a grassy meadow.

▲ Only camp at the pristine site for one night, and then move on.

▲ If you are traveling with pack stock or in a large group, avoid camping in pristine areas altogether.

Managing Timber and Trails

With roots in the 1891 Forest Reserve Act, the U.S. Forest Service was established in 1905 and is the steward of some 191 million acres of national forest and grasslands. Promoting the national forests as the "land of many uses," the Forest Service has always followed a multiple-use mandate and managed its vast reserves for the purposes of logging, mining, grazing, wildlife preservation, and recreation. Unlike other land management agencies, the Forest Service is administered by the U.S. Department of Agriculture—a branch of the federal government originally designed to focus on harvesting commodities rather than providing recreation. Although timber leases have historically been the agency's primary activity, the extent to which these nearly 200 million acres are used (and sometimes abused) to meet industry demands for a ready supply of lumber has varied greatly over the years.

Under the direction of the Forest Service's first agency chief, Gifford Pinchot, timber leasing policies were established to promote wise use of resources and the notion of a "sustainable yield." Conservation-oriented Forest Service managers such as Aldo Leopold and Robert Marshall convinced the agency during its early days to manage some of its lands as wilderness—keeping it roadless and, essentially, unlogged. By 1939, the Forest Service had set aside 14 million acres to be preserved as "primitive areas."

However, in the decades following World War II, the postwar housing boom and American society's infatuation with a new consumerism led to rampant logging of the national forests. The agency's policy of conservation-oriented sustainable yield gave way to environmentally destructive timber quotas, which led to widespread clear-cutting practices and the subsequent destruction of watersheds and fisheries. Between 1950 and 1959, for example, the annual timber harvest quota on national forest lands went from 3.5 billion board feet to more than 8 billion board feet. However, during that same period, the annual tally of recreation visits to national forests also increased dramatically—from 26 million to 81 million.

The Forest Service once considered recreation a secondary use in the agency's multiple-use mandate. But over the last several decades, sheer numbers have forced the agency to think—and act—otherwise. In 2000, recreation visits to national forest lands totaled more than 900 million, up from 600 million in 1991. Encompassing more trails, campgrounds, and waterways than any other type of federally managed land, the national forests are an increasingly popular playground for all recreational users, from backpackers to mountain bikers to boaters to hunters.

On the positive side, this has helped prompt a shift in management of national forest lands away from aggressive logging practices (hiking and clear-cutting do not mix) toward policies that are aimed at pleasing the general public rather than a few timber companies.

On the downside, the growing popularity of these lands has presented land managers with a new environmental dilemma: how to keep people from loving the national forests to death. For the Forest Service, educating all kinds of users in the principles of Leave No Trace is the agency's best hope in dealing with this problem.

Choosing a Site in Pristine Areas

If you are fortunate enough to visit a wildland area that is truly pristine—where signs of human passage are few and far between, or completely absent—then the rules of finding the perfect Leave No Trace campsite are different.

Say you are hiking cross-country in a large wilderness area in the Southwest, or in a national wildlife preserve in Alaska; it is doubtful you will encounter a well-used campsite. In cases like this, it is better to camp at a spot that appears to have never been used before than in an area that shows just modest signs of human disturbance—like a patch of flattened grass and scattered charcoal. Make your camp on a highly durable or resilient surface, such as slickrock or a dry, grassy meadow, and only spend one night there.

Camping in a pristine area is the ultimate Leave No Trace challenge because it is imperative that you literally leave no trace—and that is very hard to do. In fact, it is impossible if you are traveling in a large group and/or have pack stock. Consequently, for those who want to camp in a large group or who plan to have several horses in camp, it is best to visit popular areas where established campsites exist.

Camping in Groups

Although large, organized groups (twelve or more) make up a small percentage of wildland visitors, they, in a figurative—and sometimes literal—sense, seem to scream the loudest and can have the greatest environmental impact on campsites. Group size is regulated and governed by land managers in most national parks and popular Forest Service wilderness areas. However, the number of people allowed to convene at a single site remains unregulated on the vast majority of wildlands, leaving it up to the good judgment of visitors to decide where and what kind of group camping is appropriate in a specific environment.

Whether it is a Scout troop, a church group, or a wilderness education program such as Outward Bound or the National Outdoor Leadership School, an organized outing in the backcountry can be an extremely rewarding and enjoyable experience for the individuals involved—especially children. However, if the group is not skilled in the ways of minimum-impact camping, the outing can have devastating effects on the environment, not to mention ruin the wilderness experience of nearby campers.

How big is too big? There is no real answer to this subjective question. Group size is a controversial issue and the proper number varies greatly depending on who you talk to. If it is an outfitter who leads horsepack trips into western wilderness areas, he is likely to say that the common Forest Service limit of twenty-five people per party is about right. However, various surveys of individual visitors to wilderness areas show that their sense of solitude and enjoyment of their trip is significantly diminished when they encounter groups of ten or more.

"Scientific evidence does not support the notion that groups are inherently bad," states a new Leave No Trace Skills and Ethics booklet designed for groups. "What can be bad is a group's behavior. Current research indicates that the techniques a group uses and how it behaves in the backcountry are more important than its size in determining how the group will affect the land and other visitors."

In addition to emphasizing responsible LNT behavior, most NOLS courses lessen their environmental and social impact by breaking into subgroups. Course participants travel and camp in smaller groups and only periodically convene in one big group.

Meanwhile, the trend among land managers in popular recreation areas is to increasingly restrict organized groups. In the backcountry of Utah's Canyonlands National Park, group size is limited to six; in the Great Smoky Mountains of Tennessee it is eight; and in the Boundary Waters Canoe Area of Minnesota—an historical magnet for campers traveling en masse—the group size is ten, down from a previous limit of fifteen. In Arizona, Grand Canyon National Park has a maximum group size in the backcountry of eleven, and campers are relegated to sites designed specifically to handle quantity.

Campfires—To Burn or Not to Burn?

The minimum-impact battle is only half over once you find the perfect Leave No Trace campsite. Your behavior at that site—whether you are alone or in a group, in a pristine or in a well-used location—has everything to do with how the environment will fare after you have packed up and moved on. Perhaps the most significant impact-related decision you will make is whether to have a campfire. And, if you choose to have a fire, will it be of the type that minimizes potential environmental damage?

Campfires date back, almost, to the dawn of humankind, and over the millennia, it seems our affinity for this simple natural phenomenon has never cooled. Fires are an integral part of the human experience in the backcountry, serving, until recently, as the primary method for cooking and staying warm. However, with today's high-tech equipment—backpacking stoves, four-season tents, ultra-insulated sleeping bags, and winter apparel—people no longer need fires to survive when away from the comforts of civilization. Campfires now primarily meet an emotional need for nostalgia, tradition, and something comforting to stare at on a cold, dark night in the woods.

In following Leave No Trace guidelines to minimize the impact of fires in the backcountry, the simplest option is to use a camp stove and not have a fire at all. Some people call this the "star watching" approach, because when your eyes are not glued to the glowing flames of a fire, it is much easier to appreciate the cosmic wonders of a dark night sky. If you feel the need for a little illumination, candle lanterns work well, as do makeshift luminarias (put a few handfuls of sand in a plastic

Using a stove instead of a campfire at the Grand Canyon *(Photo by Elias Butler)*

bag and anchor a small, flat candle in the center) strategically placed around camp.

There is nothing inherently wrong about having a fire when camping in many backcountry locales; it is a perfectly natural, and often integral, part of the outdoor experience. But as with all wildland recreational issues, a problem arises when too many people make too many fires using outdated methods, and the landscape is damaged. In some fragile environments, such as deserts and alpine settings where plant growth is extremely slow, fires are just plain inappropriate.

Negative Impacts of Fires

Fire rings. One of the most obvious impacts of campfires is that telltale circle of rocks, to many visitors an eyesore in otherwise scenic wilderness areas that screams out to all who pass by, "Humans were here!" And, if the fortress of blackened stones is not unsightly enough, many campers seem to think the fire ring doubles as a trash bin. Items that people would not toss elsewhere on the ground are thrown into the ring (beer cans are the best example), regardless of whether there is a fire

Fire rings are always a magnet for unsightly trash. *(Photo by Mike Frick)*

going or whether the trash is even something that will burn. Fire rings also have an amazing ability to grow bigger, and to multiply; where one big daddy ring marks a backcountry campsite, you are likely to find several baby rings nearby.

Soil damage. While the charred rock menagerie of the fire ring may be unsightly, what goes on beneath the stones causes the most environmental damage. Hot fires permanently scar the landscape by altering the soil. The repeated infernos within the ring destroy organic matter and sterilize the soil as deep as 4 inches. The result is a patch of dead earth—something of a Superfund site—that will stay that way decades after the fire ring itself is gone. In popular areas where campfires are frequent, all these little dead zones add up to a substantially altered terrain.

Fuel consumption. The other problem with campfires is their insatiable appetite for wood. Look around a heavily used campsite in a forested setting and it is doubtful you will find any wood on the ground bigger than a twig. Then check out the surrounding trees; there is a good chance that all branches are stripped off below 6 feet, and some younger trees may have been chopped down entirely to feed the hungry flames. This constant consumption of fuel not only impacts the health of trees and their ability to regenerate, but the absence of downed wood takes away homes for wildlife and robs the soil of an important source of nutrients.

If there is a proliferation of campfires (especially large ones) in a wildland area over an extended period of time, the local forest ecosystem can suffer significantly. Although some people would like to believe otherwise, there is no type of environment that is less likely to be affected by fires; it all depends on the availability of wood, the concentration of use in the area, and the minimum-impact skills of the person building the blaze.

Yet, in light of all the potential environmental evils associated with campfires, it is also entirely possible to use Leave No Trace techniques—in appropriate locations—to build a cozy fire that has little or no impact on the landscape. And this is why, when it comes to discussing the issue of campfires, there is no end in sight to the debate, no right or wrong. It is sort of like the argument over abortion—some people are completely for it, others are completely against it, others say it depends on the circumstances, and all base their stance on strong personal convictions and moral values.

In October 1996 I attended a Leave No Trace training seminar held for Grand Canyon National Park staff, and the discussion about campfires was definitely the most heated of the day. As in many national parks, campfires are not allowed in the Grand Canyon backcountry, but everyone had an opinion just the same and the personal ethic regarding this combustible issue varied greatly. There was the biologist who was staunchly opposed to any kind of campfire in the wilderness and believed it an indulgent human luxury, and then there was the smoke jumper who felt that as long as an abundance of "fuel" existed, it was silly to not have a fire.

Building a Fire the LNT Way

Evaluate local regulations and the environment. If you decide to have a fire, first make sure it is legal in the area where you are camped and consider the weather conditions—campfires can suddenly turn into wildfires when it is hot, dry, and windy. The drought plaguing the West in recent years transformed numerous campfires into raging blazes that ravaged hundreds of thousands of acres of public land.

Fires in popular areas. If you are staying at an established site, your campfire decision also must be based on the availability of downed wood—there should be a lot of it, not just enough for one night's inferno. The ideal low-impact fuel is loose twigs and branches that are no thicker in diameter than your wrist. Never break branches from standing trees, even if they appear dead. For car campers, the fuel-availability problem is easily avoided and the environment is spared if you BYOW (bring your own wood) or—perhaps even better—invest in an artificial paraffin log, which burns longer and causes less mess than regular wood.

It is also important at established campsites to build your fire in the spot where most blazes have taken place. This is usually easy to determine, because these sites are almost always marked by an enduring fire ring planted smack-dab in the center of the impacted area. Leave the fire ring clean—with wood burned down to ash and free of trash—so that campers who follow will be encouraged to use the site rather than build a new one.

Fires at pristine sites. When camping in a pristine area, the two best methods for building a minimum-impact fire—if there is an abundant supply of downed wood—are in a self-contained unit such as a fire pan or on a mound. When done properly, neither the pan fire nor the mound fire should have any impact on the soil beneath it. However, because the business of burning inevitably attracts human activity and can become a campsite focal point, the fire should be located on a surface that is especially resistant to trampling. Gravel, sand, or slickrock are ideal.

The pan fire. A technique perfected and widely used by river runners, the pan fire offers the easiest and most environmentally sensitive way to get that warm glow in the backcountry. Fire pans are simply anything that serves as a flame-resistant metal tray with sides high enough (at least 3 inches) to safely contain wood and ashes. Various common household items work fine—oil drain pans, garbage can lids, and pans from backyard barbecue grills. Now that fire pans are becoming increasingly popular among backpackers, several outdoor equipment companies have begun to market packable lightweight fire pans. There is not much to making a pan fire once you have the pan—just fill the bottom with sand, gather the wood, and put it in the pan. When building the fire, prop the pan up on a few rocks to protect the surface below from any heat damage.

The mound fire. This type of fire has advantages in that you do not have to bother with packing a bulky fire pan; however, it also requires more work in camp. The tools needed are a trowel, a large stuff sack, and a ground cloth.

First, locate a source of mineral soil (gravel or sand) for building the mound; never build it on dark organic soil, as this dirt is rich with living organisms. Some of the best places to find mineral soil are dry streambeds where gravel or sand is easily accessible and the soil is frequently disturbed by flooding, or beneath the turned-over stump of a fallen tree.

Using the trowel, fill the large stuff sack (you can turn it inside out to keep it clean for other uses) with the mineral soil. Make a special note of your dig site so you can replace the soil when you tear down the fire. Then return to your campsite and lay down a small tarp or ground cloth (a plastic trash bag works fine) on the spot where you intend to have the fire. Spread the soil on the cloth, forming a circular, flat-topped mound about 6 to 8 inches thick. The thickness of the mound is critical in preventing any heat-caused damage to the surface beneath the ground cloth, and to keep the ground cloth itself from melting. The circumference of the mound should be larger than the fire to allow for the inevitable spread of coals.

As with all campfires, both pan and mound fires should be kept small, using only small scraps of wood for fuel. The wood should be burned all the way down to a fine ash to eliminate the lingering presence of charcoal. When you are ready to pack up camp, make sure the fire is completely out and then scatter the leftover ashes across a broad area away from the campsite (the ashes should be cool enough for you to run your hand through). If you built a mound fire, return the mineral soil to its original location.

The Camp Kitchen

There may not be a sink and fridge, but the so-called "kitchen" area of a campsite is the same kind of magnet for social activity and mess-making as your kitchen at home. However, unlike what goes on in your private abode, the backcountry kitchen is shared with all previous and future campers at the site—and with all wildlife living in the area. A messy kitchen spells problems, not only for you, but for people who follow you, as well as for numerous species of birds and animals that can come to depend on scrounging for scraps rather than hunting for food.

A friend of mine once spent the night with five ornery black bears because he unknowingly set up camp at an established backcountry site in eastern Arizona that had become the domain of bruin bandits. A long history of messy kitchen practices by backcountry visitors was to blame for the transformation of the wild bears into habituated camp robbers. As soon as my friend and his three buddies dropped their packs at the site and headed downriver to go fishing, the bears moved in—probably just as they did with all campers at that site.

When my friend and his companions returned later that afternoon, they found the gang of five bears tearing apart their packs and eating the contents. They tried scaring the bruins away, but the highly habituated animals did not budge. The bears continued to occupy the campsite, pillaging the area into the night. When they were done with the packs, they moved on to the bear-bagged food suspended from a tree branch and devoured that; then they pawed at the trash in the fire ring and ate the contents of a fishing tackle box. Meanwhile, my friend and his fellow campers had to spend the night on the cold ground across the stream from their occupied campsite, watching the raid from afar. The next morning, when the bears finally left the site—full of pancake mix, sausage, lead sinkers, and nylon cordura— my friend and his buddies picked up the tattered remains of their gear and hiked out with a new resolve to reform their sloppy camp habits.

The key to a clean camp is a clean kitchen. A few pointers to help you minimize your environmental impact and keep unwanted visitors away follow.

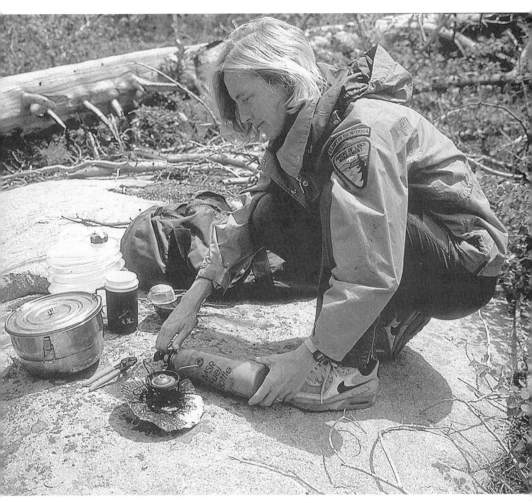

Rock is an ideal durable surface for the Leave No Trace kitchen.
(Photo courtesy of the National Outdoor Leadership School [NOLS])

Preparing Before You Leave Home

▲ Minimize mess in the camp kitchen by repackaging your food before leaving home. Take food items out of their boxes, wrappers, and cans and place them in meal-sized portions in resealable plastic bags to cut down on trash and help prevent you from cooking more grub than you want to eat.

▲ Plan your meal portions correctly so that you do not have to worry about icky leftovers. To this end, one-pot meals are the simplest to prepare, eat, and clean up.

▲ Stay away from greasy, aromatic foods. This will minimize the mess and avoid attracting wildlife.

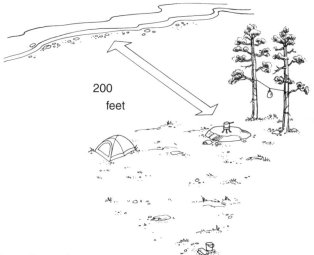

200
feet

Choosing a Location

- Find a spot for the kitchen that is well away from tents and trails, and 200 feet from water sources.
- At a pristine campsite, the cooking area should be located on trample-resistant surfaces such as a rock outcropping or mineral soil.
- At an existing campsite, concentrate use by cooking within the area that has been previously used and is visibly impacted, rather than on the periphery.
- Try to find a spot that is relatively free of debris so that if you accidentally drop food waste or trash it will be easily visible.

Food Handling

- When cooking and eating, pay close attention to and retrieve any pieces of food (even crumbs) that may drop on the ground.
- Food scraps, as well as any uneaten leftovers, should never be buried; animals will dig up your dinner discards as soon as you vacate the site (or sooner).
- Food wastes should be packed out with other garbage.

Doing the Dishes

When you are finished dining (and have eaten every last bite), do not waste any time in cleaning up, because the longer you wait, the more food particles stick to pans. The recommended Leave No Trace method for doing the dishes is to wash them with hot water and a scrubbing sponge; soap presents a potential environmental hazard and is not necessary to get dishes clean, especially if you avoid using greasy foods. After the meal, pour a little water in the dirty pot, heat it on the stove, and then take the pan to the cleanup area and scrub. There are two ways you can responsibly dispose of the "gray water," depending on which is easier for you to stomach.

Straining. The first method is to strain the water to remove the food particles; pour slowly through a small strainer, coffee filter, bandanna, or even your fingers. This is probably what you will prefer to do with the water after you've washed a dirty pot. These remaining tiny food scraps should be packed out in your trash bag, and the wastewater should be scattered in the bushes or poured into a sump (pit) well away from the campsite and 200 feet from any water sources.

Drinking. The other option is to send the liquid down the human hatch. Rinse the dish you ate out of and drink the water. It is, after all, just a little bit more of the food you ate, mixed with warm water—kind of an after-dinner broth. I have periodically partaken of this broth on backcountry outings, and it is not so bad. However, if the idea does not strike your fancy, do not hesitate to use the strain-and-scatter or sump method instead.

Taking Out the Trash

The "pack it in; pack it out" Leave No Trace practice is probably the most universally accepted part of today's minimum-impact wilderness etiquette. What is there not to understand? Simply, do not litter. Everything that you take with you into the backcountry, from chewing gum to gear, you must take out.

However, the LNT ethic involves more than just the "do not be a litterbug" decree. It has to do with making the backcountry a better place when you leave than it was when you entered. That means not only packing out your own trash, but picking up and carrying out other people's garbage, sprucing up campsites, and dismantling unnecessary fire rings.

Garbage Diehards

One devoted practitioner of the "pack it out" approach is longtime NOLS instructor Del Smith, who played an instrumental role in getting the present-day Leave No Trace program started. Smith delights in packing out other people's trash, and she and her NOLS students have been responsible for tidying up many popular wilderness areas. In camp and on the trail, Smith scours the ground for what she calls "microtrash"—teeny-weeny pieces of paper, polypropylene fuzz balls, cigarette butts. She also keeps her eyes peeled for discarded junk; if the item will not fit in her pack, she straps it to the outside. "My house is filled with junk that I have hauled out," she says. "Once I packed out a linoleum tabletop, and another time I strapped an old bale of chicken wire to my pack."

Smith is not alone in her fetish for found items; most NOLS field instructors can recount numerous odd forms of garbage they have hauled from the backcountry. Longtime field instructor Tim Wilson recalls packing out pieces of an airplane and a complete chain saw. "I once packed out three 3/4-inch iron pipes that were each about 6 feet long," reported NOLS instructor Rich Brame in a 1996 LNT training session. "It took five days, but, fortunately, there was not much lightning at the time."

Smith and other NOLS instructors admit they do not expect the average minimum-impact camper to crawl around on hands and knees looking for cigarette butts or to haul a 20-pound piece of junk out of the wilderness. It is essential, however, that you pay close attention to the goings-on of trash when you are in the backcountry.

Leaving a Clean Campsite

▲ Keep track of your own garbage by stashing it all in one bag, and stow the bag in a handy place in your pack so you can immediately get rid of discarded items instead of putting them in a pocket, only to be accidentally pulled out and blown away later. A plastic sack the size and weight of a bread bag works well for carrying garbage.

▲ When you are ready to leave a campsite, inspect the ground after you have packed all your gear to make sure you did not inadvertently leave some small item hidden in the grass or buried in the sand.

▲ When vacating a campsite in a pristine area, put some effort into erasing all signs of your stay there. Fluff the grass where the tent was located, fill in tent-stake holes, and use a fallen pine branch to sweep dirt and sand clean of footprints.

▲ If you are leaving an established site in a popular camping area, try to make the site look as appealing as possible so future visitors will not be inclined to move on to a "wilder" site. Pick up all trash and clean out the main fire ring. If there are smaller, secondary fire rings at the site, they should be dismantled. Grind charcoal down and scatter ashes in the bushes a good distance away from the site, throw any excess wood into the forest, and take the rocks from the ring and place them (black side down) throughout the area.

When Smith dismantles a fire ring, she even goes the extra mile and re-vegetates the scarred spot with organic soil and a few carefully transplanted plants from nearby. "Although it is dirty work, dismantling a fire ring and restructuring a site is really fun," she notes, contemplating her environmental zealousness. "Some people may think I am crazy, but I find that Leave No Trace ethics have a spiritual side to them."

LNT Basics: A Low-Impact Camp

Campfires

▲ Choose to not have a fire. Instead, rely on a modern backpacking stove for cooking and on good clothing, a tent, and a well-insulated sleeping bag for staying warm and dry.

▲ If you decide to have a fire, first make sure it is legal in the area where you are camped and that there is no danger of it starting a wildfire.

▲ Make sure plenty of downed wood is available for fuel. The ideal low-impact fuel is loose twigs and branches that are no thicker in diameter than your wrist; never break off branches from standing trees, even if they appear dead.

▲ At established campsites, build your fire in the primary fire ring to concentrate impact.

▲ In a pristine area where there is no fire ring, build a minimum-impact fire in a self-contained unit, such as a fire pan or on a mound.

▲ Eliminate unsightly charcoal by burning wood all the way down to ash. Once the fire is out, scatter the ash.

The Camp Kitchen

▲ At a pristine site, the cooking area should be located on trample-resistant surfaces, such as a rock outcropping or mineral soil.

▲ At an existing site, concentrate use by cooking within the area that is visibly impacted, rather than on the periphery.

▲ Keep a clean camp by avoiding dropping food on the ground and by packing out all food waste.

▲ Consider rinsing your bowl with hot water and drinking the broth—good for the environment and good for rehydration.

▲ Wash dirty pots with hot water and a scrubbing sponge; avoid using soap. Strain gray water and scatter or dump it in a sump well away from the campsite and 200 feet from any water sources.

Leave a Clean Camp

▲ Pack out all your trash, as well as litter left behind by others. Keep track of all your garbage by storing it in a single bag.

▲ Reduce trampling by wearing lightweight, flat-soled shoes such as sport sandals or running shoes when in camp.

▲ A lightweight backpacking tent is easier on the ground than the old-fashioned canvas variety.

▲ Dismantle secondary fire rings at established campsites.

▲ Fluff up the grass and fill in tent-stake holes when vacating a pristine campsite.

Chapter 3

Waste Not, Want Not
LNT GUIDELINES FOR HYGIENE
AND THE WILDERNESS BATHROOM

ome smells stay with you forever—especially the nauseating kind. There is
one such odor that permanently resides in my memory, thanks to a backpacking trip I took on a section of the Appalachian Trail in Virginia.

I was hiking as part of an organized trip, and we were camped at a
well-used site that was designated for groups. It was dusk in our little tent city
when I followed a short side trail into the bushes to find a private spot to pee. I did
my business, washed my hands, and then went back to the campsite to help prepare dinner. Sitting in front of my tent, fumbling through my food bag, I smelled
something strange, something truly putrid. It was coming from my boot.

The sun had set, but there was still enough light to see what was plastered
across the bottom of my shoe: human shit. It was fresh, so the feces smelled ripe
and were thoroughly smushed into every groove on my boot sole. Apparently some
inconsiderate person who probably had stayed at the group campsite the previous
evening did not care to properly dispose of his or her waste—or, at the very least,
to walk a decent distance from camp to do the deed.

Certainly, there are many other substances that are more toxic to humans and
the environment than human poop; smelly excreta are a natural by-product of all
warm-blooded beings. But there is something about encountering human feces in

Digging up Dirt on Human Waste in the Backcountry

Unlike campsite use or trampling on trails, human waste is not a popular topic among research biologists. There are, nevertheless, a few iron-stomached souls who have conducted limited research on the subject.

One such effort took place in the 1970s and was part of a wilderness impact study commissioned by the Sierra Club. The nonprofit environmental organization wanted to find out what impact its organized Sierra Club Outings backcountry trips had on California's Sierra Nevada mountains.

To that end, a group of researchers observed (from afar) the defecation practices of Sierra Club Outings participants—most of whom were traveling in large groups and using latrines to do their business. The group leader would usually determine where the latrine was to be dug, and the big hole was then the receptacle of all the group's poop for, in most cases, less than twenty-four hours. The researchers made a note of these latrine sites scattered across the Sierras, then they went back anywhere from one to three years later and uncovered the stinking deposits to see how the feces was faring.

Those doing the digging and subsequent observing were surprised to find that the buried treasure, along with many of its resident bacterial cooties, was alive and well and had decomposed very little—if at all. "The commonplace assumptions about decomposition are simply not borne out by the actual unearthing of latrines, even after one or two years," said the report on the foul findings, noting that the popular assumption among "public health authorities" was that latrine contents generally decompose in a month or two. "No pronounced evidence of putrefaction was found. The material looked more or less like surface privy excreta, and it still possessed the typical odor of old excreta."

Another study conducted about a decade later in Montana's Bridger Range unearthed the same stinking truths—except this time the primary fecal focus was on cat holes. Researchers from Montana State University in Bozeman buried bacteria-rich deposits of human poop in cat holes that varied in depth from 2 to 8 inches and were located in six different types of Rocky Mountain soil environments and elevations. When the samples were dug up fifty-one weeks later, after one winter had passed, all the feces remained a virtual playground for various disease-causing bacteria (namely *E. coli* and *salmonella*).

"The idea that shallow burial renders feces harmless in a short time is fallacious," said a report from the researchers, titled "Potential Health Hazards from Human Wastes in Wilderness." The report continued: "Site did not make the difference we expected. The results seemed to apply to all elevations and exposures on this mountain." The researchers went on to conclude: "From our data, it is unrealistic to hope for a rapid die-off of intestinal bacteria in cat holes. Pathogens might be transferred to later campers in three ways: by direct contact with feces, by insects, or by water." Both studies pointed out, however, that putting poop in a cat hole was preferable to a latrine because the smaller the fecal deposit, the greater its contact with surrounding soil organisms and air, which are central to the decomposition process.

Perhaps most alarming is a recent study by Nadia Kimmel, a Northern Arizona University graduate student and program director of Desert Mountain Medicine. From 2000–2002, Kimmel diligently unearthed cat hole deposits in the popular Paria River canyon of southern Utah. Not only did she find that human waste was still intact and the bacteria active, but the crap was polluting the water. This is due, in part, to the fact that the arid climate does not promote decomposition, but also because the narrow canyon of the Paria makes it difficult for people to find a cat hole spot 200 feet from water. "The water quality in the Paria was poor during our study," says Kimmel. "In some cases it was ten times the EPA standard for what's considered safe for humans." Kimmel's research has led Paria land managers to encourage visitors to pack out their poop in provided plastic bags.

Meanwhile, backcountry visitors can take solace in knowing that their urine is pretty benign. In the United States, human urine may smell rank when it accumulates in an urban alley, but it is seldom the carrier of any serious micro-cooties. As for its impact to wildlands, one industrious graduate student in California conducted research on how urine affects subalpine plants in the Sierras. Daniel Holmes concluded, after pouring 200-milliliter doses of urine over twenty-one different plant species, that "the extent of urine damage to plants in backcountry camp areas appears insufficient to be considered important in [land] management."

The study did document, however, that human pee caused leaf damage and browning on some plants. And a potentially detrimental indirect impact is that certain animals are attracted to the salt in our urine and will quickly eat up plants that we have doused with pee.

the backcountry—seeing it, smelling it, and, especially, stepping in it—that is truly repulsive and can ruin a person's "wilderness experience" like nothing else. A visible buildup of people poop—and usually the accompanying toilet paper—in popular wildland areas is a danger to public health, but the thing that stinks the most is what it does to a beautiful backcountry destination on an aesthetic level.

If we are to have any clean and intact recreational lands left at all—especially the "untrammeled" kind defined in the 1964 Wilderness Act—we human visitors have to treat the land with respect and not as a dumping ground. According to a key principle of the Leave No Trace ethic, we have to "dispose of waste properly." That means dealing with our poop rather than ignoring it, not leaving toilet paper behind, and making sure our personal hygiene practices do not negatively impact the environment.

Waste Management on Public Lands

As a result of the burgeoning number of visitors to wildland areas over the last several decades, problems associated with the proliferation of poop and other human wastes pose significant challenges to land managers.

The World Health Organization estimates that the average adult produces about one liter—some two pounds' worth—of excreta (half of that is the solid kind) per day. For the sake of discussion, consider that Great Smoky Mountains National Park counted more than one hundred thousand backcountry overnight stays in 2001. If most of those visitors stayed in the park for twenty-four hours, that means more than one hundred tons of human poop and pee was bequeathed to the Smokies' backcountry in twelve months. That is, literally, a shitload of waste, considering most of it probably never left the park by means of a sewer system and, instead, lurks at this very moment beneath a shallow grave in a half million individual burial spots.

Outhouses Are In

To prevent the spread of disease from fecal pathogens and to reduce the chance that visitors will step in each other's crap, many popular national parks and wilderness areas now have outhouses or vault toilets in the vicinity of backcountry campgrounds and trailheads. According to various surveys of land managers, these established toilets can be found at about half of all national park backcountry campsites and in 40 percent of wilderness areas. There are even toilets on top of California's Mount Whitney that are serviced by helicopter.

Backpacking all day through a wilderness area, only to find a smelly portable toilet at your designated campsite, can be somewhat disconcerting. But such is the reality of wilderness travel in a world where, in the words of NOLS instructor Rich Brame during a 1996 LNT training seminar, "Wildlands are finite, and people are infinite."

Understanding and Avoiding Potential Health Hazards

Beyond the fact that backcountry visitors do not want to see or smell human turds and urine, little is known about how our wastes affect wildland environments. It is easy to assume that if you cannot see waste, then the environmental and public health hazards are gone as well, but research suggests otherwise. The few studies that have been done on the unseemly subject have uncovered the following truths:

- ▲ Human feces buried in a group latrine can take more than three years to decompose.
- ▲ Pathogens in human feces buried in shallow cat holes can remain a potential health hazard for at least a year.
- ▲ Cat-hole disposal in narrow Southwest canyons is a health hazard because waste is slow to decompose and pollutes the water.
- ▲ Human urine can brown leaves and attract animals but, generally, it is not a health hazard.

Although you are more likely to get sick from eating a meal in a restaurant that was prepared by someone with cootie-laden hands than from exposure to human poop in the backcountry, even our nation's most pristine wilderness areas are not disease-free. A protozoon called *Giardia lamblia* inhabits most wildland waterways, and both humans and animals can be on the receiving or giving end of this fecal-to-oral-transmitted pathogen. When humans are stricken with giardiasis, they typically find it a gut-wrenching experience characterized by lots of diarrhea and

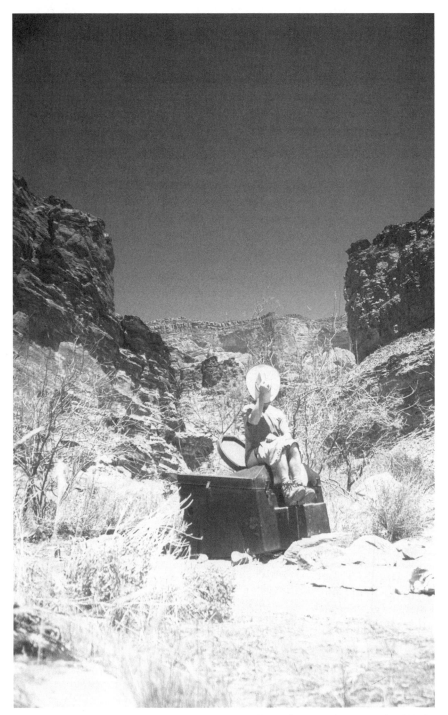

An anonymous hiker uses a backcountry toilet in the Grand Canyon. *(Photo by Mike Frick)*

Aiming to Please All Kinds of Visitors

While the management objectives of the National Park Service are not split by a multiple-use mandate as are those of the Forest Service or the Bureau of Land Management, the agency is nonetheless divided with a dual mission that is inherently contradictory. Created in 1916 by the National Parks Organic Act, the Park Service is charged with preserving our nation's crown jewels as well as enabling people to enjoy them. On the one hand, this means keeping parklands in a primitive state and undisturbed by human development. On the other hand, it means building roads, restaurants, campgrounds, and trails to accommodate the desires of the average American tourist.

From the remote 13 million–acre Wrangell–St. Elias National Park in Alaska to the White House in Washington, D.C., the Park Service manages a wide variety of national treasures—a total of 365 "units" in all. However, much of the 80 million acres of federal land placed under the agency's stewardship is found in its fifty-four national parks and eighty-four national monuments. These preserves generally have more recreation restrictions than Forest Service lands. They rarely allow mountain bikes or dogs on trails, and a permit must be obtained for overnight stays in the backcountry. But, like the national forests, our national parks and monuments have experienced significant increases in visitations over the last few decades, and many wilderness areas suffer from overuse. Recreation visits to National Park Service units in 2001 totaled nearly 280 million, up from 216 million in 1985.

Visitation at national parks, however, is highly concentrated, with 28 percent of all visitors going to the ten most popular units. Among the most visited sites are Great Smoky Mountains and Grand Canyon National Parks, Blue Ridge Parkway, and Lake Mead National Recreation Area.

But while Grand Canyon National Park, for example, received more than 4 million visitors in 2001, nearby Pipe Springs National Monument (also in Arizona) saw only 4000 visitors. The discrepancy between the units in revenues raised by visitor entrance fees is the source of great debate. In short, many park units cannot cover their operating costs solely through visitation and need to be subsidized by the federal government to stay open.

Conservative members of Congress have proposed closing park units that cannot pay for themselves. Meanwhile, national parks advocates have pushed lawmakers to allocate more money to the Department of the Interior budget to pay for the upkeep of our national treasures.

While no resolution is in sight, the National Park Service is currently experimenting with higher fees at the most popular units to raise badly needed revenue for the agency. The admission fee to Grand Canyon and Yosemite National Parks, for example, doubled in 1997 from ten dollars to twenty dollars per vehicle. When the fee increases were initiated in 1996 they were described by the agency as "temporary," but Congress is considering making the system permanent. Whether the increased fees will solve all the National Park Service's problems is doubtful. In the end, preservation of our parks will require lawmakers to see past the issue of dollars and cents and remember why these special places were set aside in the first place.

nausea. Less powerful bacteria and viruses also inhabit backcountry waters and can cause intestinal afflictions in humans (often known as "Trekker's Trots"), as can poor hygiene practices among fellow campers.

This all boils down to a need for understanding basic differences between places where there are flush toilets and water faucets, and places where there are not. In order to avoid becoming ill from fecal-borne cooties when visiting the sewerless backcountry:

▲ Purify water before drinking it.

▲ Wash your hands after doing the deed and before preparing food.

▲ Give your solid wastes a proper burial.

The Scoop on What to Do with Your Poop

Comfortably and responsibly disposing of our own feces in the backcountry is, for many people, the most difficult part of the Leave No Trace program. This is because it is a "lost art," in the words of Kathleen Meyer, author of *How to Shit in the Woods*. "Generally, a city-bred adult can expect to be no more successful than a tottering one-year-old in dropping his or her pants to squat," wrote Meyer. "Shitting in the woods is an acquired rather than innate skill, a skill honed only by practice, a skill all but lost to the bulk of the population, along with the arts of making soap, carding wool, and skinning buffalo."

Plan Ahead

As part of your preparation for any backcountry trip, come up with a poop plan. Maybe this is something you can take for granted in the city, but anticipating how you are going to dispose of your waste in the wilds, and bringing along the necessary tools to successfully accomplish the mission, makes the whole process less stressful, more efficient, and, dare I say, reasonably enjoyable.

First, contact the appropriate land manager and find out what the rules are regarding waste disposal in the area you will be visiting. If you are camping or hiking in an area where toilets are provided, hold your nose and use them. In these places, land managers have decided that heavy visitation warrants the installation of a toilet because it is better to concentrate the waste in one strategically located spot than to have campers digging up each other's cat holes.

Some people like the convenience of having an established place to poop located a short walk from their tent; others feel the synthetic intrusion interferes with their wilderness experience. If you do not like the idea of doing your business in an outhouse and would rather gaze out at a beautiful panorama when answering nature's call, then steer clear of heavily visited backcountry destinations. Most parks and wilderness areas that require visitors to obtain a permit and camp at designated sites are likely to have designated toilets as well.

If outhouses or vault toilets are not provided, chances are the management policy is for campers to dig a cat hole and to pack out their toilet paper. Other methods used in special circumstances include packing out the poop, digging a latrine, smearing (also called surface disposal), and something known as a "shit put," where the goods are deposited on a rock and hurled into the abyss—usually off a glacier. (More information on appropriate alternative waste-disposal methods for specific types of users or environments follows in Chapters 4–7.)

According to Leave No Trace guidelines, there are three main objectives to consider when deciding how and where to dispose of your poop:

▲ Minimize the chance that other people and/or animals will find it.
▲ Minimize the chance that nearby waters could be polluted.
▲ Maximize the rate of decomposition.

The Art of the Cat Hole

The cat hole is the most widely used and the best option in most situations. As in real estate sales, the key to achieving pooping perfection when using a cat hole: location . . . location . . . location.

For starters, the cat hole should be located at least 200 feet from any water sources, campsites, and trails. But there are also aesthetic factors to consider when deciding where to dig. The site should entertain the squatter with an inspiring view (anything from a quiet forest scene to a sweeping mountain panorama); it should be intensely private, without any worries of being spotted by other humans; and it must be comfortable—not on a steep slope or swarming with fire ants, for example. Additionally, maximum conditions for decomposition will be achieved if the hole is dug in organic soil (rich in microorganisms) and in a spot that is somewhat moist but receives a fair amount of sunlight.

Now, after taking a short morning hike to get your bowels moving and to find the prime cat-hole site, it is time to dig the hole. You will need some kind of trowel—there is the standard orange plastic shovel, which has been known to break in rocky or frozen ground; a basic gardening trowel will do; or you can purchase a stainless-steel shovel with a collapsible handle and sturdy carrying case, called the "Cadillac of trowels" by *Backpacker* magazine. The cat hole should be about 4 to 8 inches deep and 4 to 6 inches in diameter.

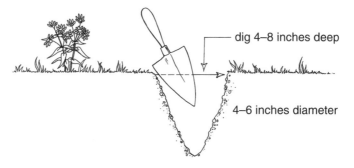

dig 4–8 inches deep

4–6 inches diameter

Some people are natural squatters; others have a hard time relaxing and holding their balance when straddling a small hole. If you are one of the latter, try sitting on a fallen log (look out for the ants) or on a flat-topped rock, and hang your buns off the end, resting strategically above the hole you just dug. Or hold on to a sturdy branch or rock to take the pressure off your legs when in the squatting stance. However, hold on tight because there is nothing worse than losing your balance and falling backward into the hole after you have made a deposit.

Once you have done the deed, throw a little soil in the hole for good measure and stir the stuff with a stick to speed up decomposition, and throw the stick in too. Then use your trowel to place at least 2 inches of topsoil back in the hole and camouflage the excavation site. (Diluting poop with a little water from your water bottle may help minimize smells.)

When to Make a Latrine

Although dispersing buried fecal waste across a broad area through the use of cat holes is generally preferable to concentrating it in a latrine, sometimes digging a big poop pit is your best option. This is the case, for example, if you are camping with a group of children who do not have the ability to properly dig their own cat holes—and somehow you neglected to pick a campsite with an outhouse. A latrine also may be appropriate for a group that will be staying more than one or two nights at a popular backcountry site with no outhouse.

Dig the latrine when you first get to camp and make sure everyone knows where it is. The hole must be at least 200 feet from any water sources or drainages, and should be wider than it is deep—it should be at least 1 foot deep. Make the hole rectangular to accommodate squatting. Or, if your group has the packing capacity, bring in some type of toilet seat device to place over the hole. Soil should be thrown in the hole after each use, and the latrine should be covered with dirt when the waste accumulation is within 4 to 6 inches of the surface.

If you anticipate that you may be in a situation where digging a latrine might be necessary, consider the better minimum-impact option of camping in an area where outhouses are provided, or bring along a portable group potty (see Chapter 7, "Minimizing Impacts on Waterways," for more details on these products).

Surface Disposal

Surface disposal—commonly known as smearing—was all the rage among LNT aficionados in the early '90s. This unlikely method involves pooping on a flat, inorganic surface, such as slickrock, and then spreading it across the surface with a stick or stone, as if icing a cake. This modus operandi came into vogue as the result of field observations that feces exposed to sunlight and warmth decomposed and virtually disappeared within several days. But the folks who pioneered this approach to pooping also emphasized that one should only engage in smear tactics in

Toilet at the Hermit Creek campsite, Grand Canyon *(Photo by Elias Butler)*

extremely remote locations, well away from trails, and where there is a very dry, sunny climate—like in the Southwest desert, in the Rockies above tree line, or in the northern reaches above the Arctic Circle, where the ground (if you can get to it) is too frozen for digging.

"My first three summers at NOLS I worked in Alaska," recalls NOLS Leave No Trace program coordinator Michael Cheek. "At that time we used smearing almost exclusively in tundra environments, but it was very hard to get students to do it properly. I would now advocate the smearing technique only when it is not possible to use a cat hole."

Aside from the aesthetic consequences of someone else seeing it, smearing poses health risks for those who follow in the footsteps of the smearer. Fecal pathogens can be picked up and transported by insects, carried on the wind, or washed by rain or snowmelt into waterways. There are places where this type of surface disposal may, nevertheless, meet LNT objectives more effectively than burial, but such locations are few and far between.

Packing It Out

In places where waste burial is not possible or environmentally advantageous, packing out your poop may the best (or only available) evacuation route. Land management policy for many popular whitewater rivers in the West, such as the Colorado River through Grand Canyon National Park, dictates that all solid wastes be carried out via portable potties. Climbers in Yosemite National Park, Grand Teton National Park, and Mount Shasta and hikers through the narrows of Zion National Park are also required to pack it out. Among the methods used are plastic bag systems (WAG Bag and Restop 2, for example) and a simple PVC pipe contraption called a "poop tube" (see Chapter 7, "Minimizing Impacts on Waterways," for information on constructing this ingenious device).

Even if packing it out is not required by land managers, there may be places where, because of high visitation or an extremely sensitive environment, you decide that taking your waste with you rather than leaving it behind is the most responsible thing to do. Such is the case for LNT-minded hikers in the crowded narrows of Utah's Paria Canyon, where human waste is polluting the river, and for kayakers traveling the Maine Island Trail who want to minimize human impacts on the tiny barrier islands where paddlers camp. Many of these poop-packers have pioneered their own techniques—like using a Tupperware container and kitty litter, or a system of poop-filled paper bags stored in resealable plastic bags. Keep in mind, however, that no matter how you pack it, all poop must ultimately be deposited (without non-biodegradable plastic bags and/or containers) in a proper human-waste-disposal site—such as an RV dump station or outhouse.

TP, Pee, and Other Hygienic Hang-Ups

Certainly, knowing how to effectively deal with your poop is the major hurdle when it comes to backcountry hygiene, but there are other concerns when traveling in a world without plumbing. For instance, what about wiping?

The Tissue Issue

In our everyday, flushable environs, toilet paper is part and parcel of the evacuation process. However, in the backcountry, it poses an environmental dilemma. You should avoid burying it, because it decomposes very slowly and animals like to dig it up. You should not burn it because land managers will tell you that more wildfires have been started by flaming TP than they care to count. This leaves two responsible minimum-impact options when it comes to the tissue issue: either pack it out or leave it at home and use wipes provided by nature.

The whole business of toilet paper is entirely discretionary. After all, people were pooping long before double-quilted TP was invented. But on the other hand, our modern-day bottoms have been conditioned since birth to be well

Natural wipes:

river stone

seaweed

snow

moss

fir cone

large leaf

wiped, and slacking off in this area can lead to uncomfortable skin irritations.

Traveling sans TP does not mean you should abandon the practice of wiping, but that you should become an educated user of the many tissue alternatives available in the great outdoors. I know numerous people who are enthusiastic connoisseurs of natural wiping materials. In desert and river environs, one hiker swears by palm-sized, smooth sandstone; another friend, who spends more time in the mountains, sings the praises of fallen leaves, and when they are available in abundant quantities, he will enjoy the luxurious pampering of a woolly mullein leaf or two. Other organic options include snowballs, soft cones from fir trees, and seaweed. As a general minimum-impact rule, it is best to reach for something that is already on the ground instead of defoliating a live plant. When you are done wiping, put whatever you used into the cat hole to be buried with the rest of your offerings.

If experimenting with nature's various tissue alternatives does not appeal to you, the "mitten method" is a tidy way to keep soiled TP out of the backcountry—and it keeps you from having to touch it. To pack out toilet paper using this hands-off approach, you will need a well-stocked supply of medium-sized, open-top plastic sandwich bags and one large resealable bag.

After doing your duty in the cat hole and replacing the soil, use a conservative amount of TP (you still have to pack it out) and throw it on the ground. Then take one of the open-top plastic bags and invert it like a mitten over your hand. Pick up the toilet paper, using the "mitten," and pull the bag right-side out over the soiled tissue. The tissue is now in its own self-contained storage unit; place it inside the large resealable bag. If you really want to improve the aesthetics of the process, use an opaque resealable bag for storing the TP so you do not have to look at it, and occasionally use a perfumed towelette to hide the smell of the TP stash. Then carry all your TP supplies in their own designated ditty bag so you will know what you are pulling out of your pack. No one wants to get their TP bag when they thought they were reaching for lunch.

Women's Hygiene

For menstruating women, the mitten method—or a less elaborate baggie system—suffices to pack out tampons and other items. Carrying these out of the backcountry is the only responsible LNT option and, although it may seem like an unpleasant hassle at first, once you get a system down, it becomes second nature. Perfumed towelettes are especially handy during these times for cleaning purposes and for keeping the stash in the baggie smelling fresh. Other methods for absorbing odors include placing a crushed aspirin or a used tea bag (herbal or black will do) in the stuff being packed out.

Baby Diapers

If you have a baby along, regardless of your diaper preferences, scrape off as much poop as possible with a stick and bury it in a cat hole. Be prepared to pack out all disposable diapers. If you use nondisposables, wash them out 200 feet away from water sources. Rinsing diapers can be problematic because they contaminate the rinse container you use, but this is no excuse to contaminate a water source. Just carry the poopy rinse container in a secured plastic bag and keep it away from all food and utensils.

A Few Pointers About Pee

Compared to human waste concerns of the solid kind, peeing in the backcountry is a simple affair. Human urine in the well-vaccinated United States poses minimal threats in terms of disease, and it is quickly absorbed into the soil where it is deposited. However, when picking a place to pee, keep in mind that animals are attracted to the salts in our urine and if you happen to water some plants, critters will soon come and defoliate them. Diluting urine with a little water from your water bottle may help minimize salty problems. Also, avoid peeing in areas where others might camp.

Men have it easiest—just aim with the wind and keep the spray away from vegetation and trails. Women, meanwhile, must squat and be concerned with not splattering their boots. I have found that sand or a bed of pine needles absorbs the force of oncoming liquid with little or no repercussions. In any peeing incident, make sure you are at least 200 feet away from water sources. Drip-drying requires no TP at all; all-natural TP is preferable to paper because paper needs to be carried out.

Bathing

Things that we often do at least once a day in our regular sanitary existence—putting on clean clothes, taking a shower, washing our hair—are all optional in the backcountry. (They could be more optional at home as well; see the Adopting a LNT Lifestyle section in Chapter 9, "Sharing the LNT Message.") When it comes to minimizing human impact in our precious wildlands, the less soap, the better.

"Bacteria building up on the body can really stink but it's not a serious hygienic issue," says veteran backpacker William Forgey, M.D., president of the Wilderness Medical Society. "It's far more important, from a health standpoint, to thoroughly wash your hands and dishes than your armpits."

The only bathing practice that should not be considered optional is regularly washing your hands—especially after visiting a cat hole or before preparing a meal. In fact, you can go for two weeks without washing your hair and it will not affect a soul, but failure to wash your hands just once could pass along a parasite that makes everyone in camp sick.

As with all washing activities, clean your hands at least 200 feet away from water sources. Carry a bottle of water or (ideally) a pot of warm water away from the water source, preferably to a durable surface such as gravel or slickrock. Wet your hands, use a small amount of phosphate-free, biodegradable soap, lather up, and rinse by pouring water over your hands, not by dipping your hands into the pot of water. Avoid any contamination of soap on cooking utensils, as the soap can give you diarrhea. Alcoholic hand-sanitizer gel offers extra germ-busting power when used after and between washings but should not be considered a replacement for a good scrub. If you choose to wash your hair or bathe, this same method should be used. Bathing in a large lake, stream, or river is acceptable by LNT standards, if you do not use soap. And if you swim in your clothes, you can wash them (without soap) at the same time.

It is unrealistic to expect to feel squeaky-clean when visiting the backcountry. However, everyone has to find their own hygienic comfort level and determine what practices they can and cannot give up. I know one person who is the most

Enjoying backcountry waters *(Photo by Robert Kozlow)* ▶

rugged of wilderness travelers in every respect, except for the fact that he becomes grumpy if he does not wash his hair every day, whereas I have to put on clean socks and brush my teeth every morning. (You can minimize the impact of oral hygiene by using salt or baking soda instead of toothpaste; spray spit through your teeth, or swallow it unless it contains fluoride.)

Outdoor writer and adventurer Mark Jenkins has gone for seventy-five days in the Himalayas "without bathing of any kind." Jenkins reports that "your body reaches a state of stench equilibrium after about three weeks; you won't smell any worse after nine weeks in the wilds than you do after three. As long as your comrades in mischief stink as bad as you do, no worries. It's only when some sour puss can't take it anymore and decides to use a bar of soap that everything goes to hell."

There may even be benefits to stinking. "The more you wash off your body odor, the more you attract insects," adds Forgey. "The stink is a natural detractor."

Health Precautions

▲ Boil or filter and treat water before drinking it.

▲ Wash your hands after pooping and/or peeing, and before preparing food.

Human Waste

▲ If there is an outhouse provided, use it to concentrate impact.

▲ In most backcountry situations where there is no outhouse, burying your waste in a shallow cat hole is the best disposal method.

▲ Cat holes should be located at least 200 feet from any water sources, campsites, and trails.

▲ Maximum conditions for decomposition are achieved when the hole is dug in organic soil (rich in microorganisms) and in a spot that is somewhat moist but receives a fair amount of sunlight.

▲ Use a trowel to dig a hole that is about 6 to 8 inches deep and 4 to 6 inches in diameter.

▲ Once you have made a deposit, throw in some soil and stir the stuff with a stick. Then place at least 2 inches of topsoil back in the hole and camouflage the site.

▲ Dig a latrine if you are camping in a large group that is staying at the same site several nights or that contains young children who are not capable of digging a cat hole.

▲ Pack out all toilet paper, or avoid the hassle by using a natural wiping alternative such as snow, leaves, or river stones.

▲ Tampons and disposable diapers must be packed out as well.

▲ Avoid urinating on plants because animals are attracted to the salty liquid.

Bathing

▲ With the exception of hand washing, bathing should be considered optional in the backcountry because it has unavoidable environmental consequences.

▲ Any washing activities should take place at least 200 feet from natural water sources and preferably on a durable surface such as gravel or slickrock.

▲ If you use soap, make sure it is phosphate-free and biodegradable.

▲ If you do not use soap, washing in a natural body of water is acceptable by LNT standards only in a large lake or river.

▲ Minimize tooth-brushing contamination by using salt or baking soda instead of toothpaste.

Chapter 4

Getting Along with Man and Beast

LNT GUIDELINES FOR MINIMIZING YOUR IMPACT ON FELLOW WILDERNESS TRAVELERS AND WILDLIFE

It was my first backpacking trip in the Grand Canyon. As we began to descend the Hermit Trail from the canyon's south rim, I was so excited I had a hard time not slipping on the steep, rocky path. Soon the trail would break out from the narrow Hermit Creek drainage and open up to what I expected would be the most spectacular vista I'd ever seen. In just another half-mile we'd be there.

Then we heard something strange. We stopped to listen more closely. It was definitely not the wind or an animal. It was people—screaming. As we got closer to the trail's first broad canyon panorama, we realized the four-member hiking party about a half-mile ahead of us was standing at the overlook as if they were in the stands of a football stadium watching a touchdown. They were whooping and hollering at the top of their lungs.

"The Screamers," as we nicknamed the group, proceeded to let out big whoops (while punching the air and hugging each other) at every overlook along the trail. For four hours, while descending 5000 feet into one of our nation's most spectacular natural wonders, we heard the kind of yelling you only expect at a sporting event. Obviously, "the Screamers" were excited about their first hike in the Grand Canyon. But so was I. And the noise they created ruined what I expected to be a quiet, awe-inspiring wilderness experience.

We humans can really get on each other's nerves. Even in the wilderness—where many people go for the purpose of getting away from fellow humans—there are often people who annoy. And it's even worse for wildlife. Not only do humans (often unknowingly) annoy the creatures living in the wildlands we visit, but we can threaten the animals' very existence by infringing on their habitat and screwing up their natural cycles. Unfortunately, as visitation to wildlands increases, so do the social and wildlife conflicts in the places that were once thought to be free from such human-caused problems.

In 1999, the Leave No Trace Education Review Committee revised the program's basic principles to directly address impacts to human visitors and to wildlife. The principles "be considerate of other visitors" and "respect wildlife" were added to the wilderness code of conduct. Although the "golden rule," so to speak, was implied in the original principles, LNT leaders wanted to make it a more prominent part of the Leave No Trace ethic. In a world where the human population keeps getting bigger and undisturbed backcountry keeps getting smaller, we have to be sensitive about how our presence in wilderness affects not only the landscape but also the creatures within it.

Do Unto Others . . .

The Golden Rule (do unto others as you would have them do unto you) is something most of us learn by the time we're in kindergarten, but people have a tendency to forget it in the backcountry. Sure, one of the great things about wilderness camping is you can leave many social constraints at the trailhead—bathing, table manners, work responsibilities—but common courtesy is not one of them. Even though you will hopefully encounter far fewer people on a backcountry excursion than you would in town, you are still sharing the place with others.

According to research cited in *Studies in Outdoor Recreation* by Robert Manning, two-thirds of all wilderness areas were described by land managers as "beyond capacity" in certain places during popular visitation times. "In most of these cases (53 percent)," writes Manning, "overuse problems were considered to be of a social or crowding nature as opposed to resource damage." Unfortunately, there are very few wilderness areas in the Lower 48 where you can be truly alone for extended periods. The reality of backcountry recreation in the twenty-first century is that we're all in this together and we've got to get along.

Of course, getting along would be much simpler if we all had the same goals and expectations on a wilderness trip. But they vary as much as the individual personalities of people visiting the wilderness. Some recreationists head into the

Hikers stumble upon an abandoned, trashed campsite in Great Smoky Mountains National Park. *(Photo by Steve Howe)*

To Hike or Not to Hike with Rover

Although pets are banned from most national park trails, it is common to see people traveling and camping with their dogs in most other wildland areas. For the dog, roaming about in the backcountry is a great thrill and beats a boring city park any day. However, bringing these domestic animals into a wild area often disturbs other users and has a negative impact on the environment. Dogs chase other people's dogs, they harass wildlife (which can have serious consequences for a threatened species such as bighorn sheep), they bark, they disrupt water sources, and they defecate on the trail and at campsites.

A well-behaved dog in camp *(Photo by Annette McGivney)*

But with all this being said, some people (women backpacking alone, for instance) find that a well-trained dog is a faithful trail companion and is worth taking the extra precautions to minimize the animal's impact on the environment. If after weighing the pros and cons, you decide to take your dog with you into the backcountry, follow these guidelines to keep your dog and its inevitable consequences in check:

▲ Try to choose a rarely visited destination where there will be little chance of contact with other users.
▲ Regardless of where you are, keep your dog on the trail and restrained from chasing wildlife.
▲ Restrain your dog from barking at and jumping up on other hikers.
▲ When your furry friend leaves a little doggie pile, pull out your trowel and bury it away from the trail and water sources in a cat hole just as you would human feces.

- ▲ Instead of allowing your dog to romp through springs and ponds—which will likely scare area wildlife away from a critical water source for some time—scoop the water into a bowl and let Fido lap it up 200 feet away.
- ▲ Prevent your dog from defecating in water. Dogs, like beavers and other animals, can carry *Giardia* and thus can contaminate water.
- ▲ In camp, keep your dog restrained or have it trained to stay within the site; a wandering dog will disturb wildlife and perhaps other campers.
- ▲ Dog food is very aromatic and will attract wildlife. Secure it with your own food.
- ▲ Prevent your dog from barking.

backcountry alone with the sole desire to get away from people, while others are there to socialize with their friends. Some people want quiet; others want conversation. Some people prefer to hike to their destination, while others travel via mountain bike or horseback. Some recreationists like to bring their dogs; other people hate dogs. And everybody wants to camp and hike in the same places. It all adds up to one big headache for land managers who are charged with resolving visitor crowding and conflict issues.

"The perception of wilderness is relative—it varies from one individual to another—but there's been enough research done now that we've discovered some commonalities," social scientist Marty Lee of Northern Arizona University's College of Ecosystem Science Management tells me. "It's not just the numbers of visitors encountered that makes people feel crowded in wilderness. There are other variables."

First and foremost, the behavior of other people determines whether or not a wilderness visitor feels "crowded." On my first hike in the Grand Canyon, for example, the only other people we saw on the Hermit Trail were the four "Screamers." But because of their obnoxious behavior, that was four too many. I would have been much happier about encountering twenty quiet hikers. Another commonality among wilderness visitors, according to Lee, is that people don't mind sharing the trail with others (as long as they're not screaming), but they do mind sharing a campsite. Experienced backpackers prefer solitude, while novice hikers "are usually glad to find one other party where they're camping."

A 1995 survey by William Hammitt and William Rutlin (reported in *Leisure Sciences*) of six hundred visitors to South Carolina's Ellicott Rock Wilderness found that the "ideal" number of groups they'd like to encounter on the trail during their trip is 3.7 and "maximum" (verging on negatively impacting their experience) is 8.6. Meanwhile, in camp their "ideal" number is one group encounter and "maximum" is 2.4.

"Land managers used to just be concerned about environmental impacts caused by visitors," observes Lee. "Now they need to also worry about impacts to visitor experiences. It's part of their management mission." In fact, managers are required by law under the Wilderness Act to preserve "opportunities for solitude" in designated wilderness areas. Even though solitude to one person may mean not seeing another soul for a week, while someone else experiences a sense of solitude on a fifteen-member rafting trip, managers have to find a way for all visitors to attain that elusive solitary experience. Technically, if a person doesn't feel a sense of solitude in a place, then it doesn't meet the definition of "wilderness" in the Wilderness Act.

Something for Everyone

Realistically, our wildlands, from a recreational standpoint, cannot be all things to all people. But land managers do their best to please as many people as possible with a management strategy called the Recreation Opportunity Spectrum. Under this approach, a wilderness area and/or national park is divided into different zones

A crowded trail in California's Trinity Wilderness *(Photo by Dennis Lewon)*

that cater to recreational interests and various definitions of solitude. The method also helps land managers concentrate impact by sending the highest number of visitors to the most heavily used places.

Grand Canyon National Park has used a Recreation Opportunity Spectrum strategy to manage its backcountry since 1988. The park is split into four zones: the "corridor," which contains the two most heavily used rim-to-river trails and sees the vast majority of hiker traffic, especially day hiking; the "threshold," with several increasingly popular trails; the "primitive," with more rugged trails and less traffic; and the "wild areas," with little or no trails and very infrequent visitation because of the remote, rugged terrain. The "corridor" and "threshold" zones generally have designated campsites and vault toilets, while the "primitive" and "wild areas" allow at-large camping and have no facilities. The number of people allowed in the various zones at any one time is regulated by the park's permit process. Far more people are allowed in the "corridor" and "threshold" zones than in the "primitive" and "wild areas." For example, I've encountered more than one hundred people in a single day on the park's Bright Angel Trail in the "corridor," but gone for five days in a "wild area" without seeing another party.

"We are concentrating impact and providing for a range of opportunities," explains Grand Canyon Recreation Resources Planner Linda Jalbert. "The 'corridor' is in non-wilderness. The numbers of people get progressively lower as you go from 'corridor' to 'wild.'" When visitors apply for a backcountry permit, Grand Canyon staff "educate" them on the various levels of wilderness experience available in the park. "If they're new to the canyon or to backpacking, we try to steer them to the 'corridor.' And we try to give them an idea of what to expect there," says Jalbert. "The experienced hikers are requesting to go to the more remote areas. They're willing to make the journey for solitude."

Code of Conduct

But even the best land management strategies have limitations. Jalbert admits that the Grand Canyon's "corridor" and "threshold" zones are getting hammered, and visitors complain about crowding and conflicts. So what's the solution? Responsible, considerate behavior among wildland users must pick up where the land management strategy leaves off. To that end, follow these guidelines to promote the LNT principle, "be considerate of other visitors":

▲ Avoid disappointments and potential conflicts with other visitors by researching the "recreation opportunity spectrum" before your trip. If your goal is to encounter no one, check with land managers to see if the odds are likely for that in the place you want to visit. If you're a hiker and dislike encounters with horses, try to visit a place that's not popular with equestrians. If you're seeking peace and quiet, don't go to a popular place on a popular weekend.

Friendly campers ready to share their shelter on the Appalachian Trail
(Photo by Robert Kozlow)

- ▲ Yield to others. If you're a hiker or mountain biker, step to the downhill side of trail and let a horse party pass. People hiking or biking downhill should yield to those huffing and puffing uphill. Mountain bikers should slow down for hikers. If you are going to pass someone, first announce your presence. In general, practice common courtesy. (For more on trail etiquette, see Chapters 5 and 6 on hiking, mountain biking, and horseback riding.)
- ▲ Respect boundaries. You may be on "public" land, but let people have their own space. Don't walk through another person's campsite on your way to the toilet. Close ranch gates after passing through and don't disturb fences. Uphold voluntary closures of public lands for Native American religious ceremonies.
- ▲ Keep a low profile. Take rest breaks a short distance from the trail on durable surfaces out of sight from other visitors. Try to camp out of sight and earshot of other visitors. Larger groups should be especially aware of their presence and not infringe on the experience of other visitors. Don't "take over" scenic overlooks and community camping areas.

▲ Let nature's sounds prevail. Don't shout on the trail or in camp. For many people, the wilderness is a place to enjoy the quiet—to hear the wind, bird song, and rustle of leaves. Yelling to get the attention of other members in your party can be very obnoxious to fellow wilderness visitors. If you bring your dog, keep it from barking in camp. If you bring music, wear headphones. Be discreet with the use of cellular phones.

▲ Avoid hostile confrontations with wildland visitors who do not share your environmental values. Increasing visitation in wilderness means you're likely to encounter situations that make you angry, but be tactful in how you communicate your displeasure. (See the "show them a better way" technique and other ways to teach not preach in Chapter 9, "Sharing the LNT Message.")

LNT Basics: Respecting Others

▲ Avoid disappointments by researching your destination before your trip. Is it known for solitude? Primitive camping? Spring Break parties?

▲ Yield to others. If you're a hiker or mountain biker, step to the downhill side of the trail and let a horse party pass. In general, practice common courtesy.

▲ Keep a low profile. Take rest breaks a short distance from the trail on durable surfaces out of sight from other visitors. Try to camp out of sight and earshot of other visitors.

▲ Let nature's sounds prevail. Don't shout on the trail or in camp. If you bring music, wear headphones. Be discreet with the use of cellular phones.

Peaceful Coexistence with Wildlife

Every seasoned wilderness traveler has camp pirate stories—outlandish tales about how wildlife outwitted humans to steal their food. One of the best stories I've heard lately is from Jeff Marion, who, as one of the nation's most respected recreation ecologists, studies wildlife impacts but is not immune to the highly skilled raiding tactics of ringtails. "We spent one night at a campsite in Zion National Park with a ringtail that managed to outwit every type of food hang we could devise," Marion told me. "We'd try one method and then sit back and watch him figure it out. He had no problem climbing across or down 1/8-inch nylon cord. On another night a ringtail went deep into my pack for a bag of gorp. The pack was under a tarp tent about 6 inches from my head, and I never woke up."

Meanwhile, I've had buzzards peck into a box of Pop-Tarts in Big Bend National Park in Texas, watched raccoons on California's Lost Coast drag away an entire stuff-sack of food, and stood disbelieving in the Grand Canyon as ravens unzipped the lid of my pack and pulled out PowerBars. Fortunately, I've never had my camp raided by bears looking for pancake mix (see "The Camp Kitchen,"

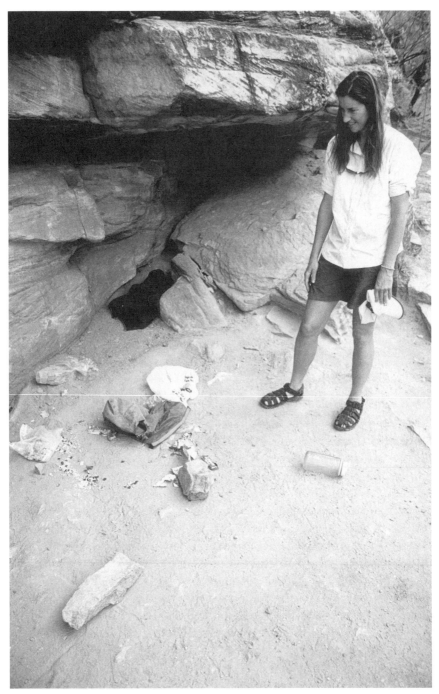

The author surveys the damage after her food bag has been raided by ravens and squirrels at Hermit Creek Camp, Grand Canyon. *(Photo by Elias Butler)*

Chapter 2). While we can laugh about being outsmarted by wily critters and enjoy retelling the humorous tales, there's nothing funny about it for the wildlife doing the raiding. If it's a bear, there's a good chance the bruin will be killed because land managers will view it as a threat to humans. For other creatures addicted to human food, a diet of M&Ms, energy bars, and bagels is hardly what nature intended.

Unfortunately for many species of wildlife in the United States, our public lands comprise the only large swaths of unaltered habitat they have left. Even without the threats posed by recreationists, the animals are struggling to survive. "The number of species in our western national parks has been declining steadily because the parks are islands in a sea of cropland, logged-over timberland, and development," observes Pulitzer Prize–winning author and biologist Edward O. Wilson. "The rule illustrated by this phenomenon is the following: as habitat is reduced in size, the number of species it can sustain falls. For example, 10 percent of the original area can support, as a general, well-documented principle, only about half the original species."

This is not to say that humans should stay out of the wilderness. Many of us need wilderness for our emotional and spiritual survival. But we must visit these precious wildland habitats in a cautious, conscientious manner that does not threaten the creatures who live there.

According to David Cole and Richard Knight in their 1991 report, "Effects of Recreational Activity on Wildlife in Wildlands," there are four primary ways people disturb animals when we're Out There. First is harvesting—which is hunting and is clearly undesirable if it's done illegally. Then there's habitat modification, which refers to altering vegetation and soils—usually along trails and in campsites—that certain species depend on for food and/or shelter. Third is pollution, which may sound obvious, but it's usually far more subtle than the *Exxon Valdez* oil spill. Every time we accidentally drop crumbs on the ground or stick our oily, sunscreen-covered hands into a water source, we pollute wildlife habitat. The fourth, and probably the most wide-ranging human-caused impact, is disturbance. When we disturb animals (often unintentionally), sometimes they just run away until we pass and then resume what they were doing. But disturbance also can cause species to move out of their preferred habitat, abandon their young, or even die from stress.

The upshot to all of this is that 99 percent of it is preventable. You don't have to drop food on the ground or chase after an animal to get a photo or camp right next to its water source. Follow these LNT guidelines to give wildlife the respect they deserve.

Don't (Accidentally) Feed the Animals

Be fastidiously clean with food waste in your camp kitchen and while eating in camp and on the trail (see Chapter 2). Keeping area wildlife from turning into junk-food junkies also requires that you carefully store your food. Although black bears are, perhaps, the most notorious for learning to associate camping and back-packing equipment with the source of their next meal, the natural habits of many species can be altered if they learn to pillage and panhandle.

In established camping areas in popular national parks, you are likely to be visited by a variety of critters—raccoons, squirrels, chipmunks, skunks, deer—all looking for a handout. In many of these places, lockboxes or other containers are provided to protect your food and the animals. Use them. Land managers will typically relocate bears gone bad who are habitual campsite raiders, but if that does not work, the bruins are often given the death sentence.

Secure All Food and Other Attractants

The best way to protect your food and gear—and the future of area wildlife—is to secure all your food, garbage, and any scented toiletries such as toothpaste, sun-screen, and lip balm. In some areas, bear-proof containers are provided for this purpose. But in most areas, especially the backcountry, you will have to hang your food in "bear-bag" fashion. Check with land managers before visiting an area to find out how elaborate your bear-bagging suspension system should be.

Here are some general guidelines for keeping your edibles out of the reach of wildlife:

- ▲ You will need anywhere from 30 to 100 feet of nylon rope and a sturdy bag or stuff-sack to hold all the goods.
- ▲ As a general rule, food should be hung from a tree (or trees) about 100 feet from your tent site. It is best to hang the food bag near the camp kitchen in an effort to keep appetizing odors concentrated in one area.
- ▲ If bear raids have not been reported, or if you know you are not in bear country, simply slinging a rope over a lofty branch and tying the bag to it will keep it out of reach of most critters.
- ▲ If you are in bear country, or especially an area where bears have been raiding campsites, spend a little bit more time rigging the food bag so that it is

suspended about 15 feet high between two trees at least 23 feet apart. This will decrease the likelihood that a black bear will try to steal your food by climbing the tree from which its prospective dinner dangles. (However, in the case of my friend who shared his camp with five bears, the bruins simply broke off the entire branch that the food bag was tied to.)

Avoid Handouts

No matter how cute the begging tactics of little critters, refrain from feeding wildlife. They are, after all, supposed to be wild, and the animals' very survival is jeopardized if they lose their instinctive ability to fend for themselves.

Be Aware of Water Sources

Regardless of whether any furry bandits enter your camp or whether you see any animals at all, be sensitive to the fact that your temporary presence inevitably

Observe wildlife from a distance. *(Photo by Robert Kozlow)*

affects area wildlife. If you are camped near a water source (at least 200 feet away, of course), try to minimize the disruption you may cause to wildlife watering habits by visiting the spring or stream only once. This can be most easily accomplished if you pack a collapsible water jug, then take it with you to the water source and pump or extract all the water you will need in camp in one visit, rather than make repeated trips to what is undoubtedly a critical spot for wildlife.

Observe from a Distance

One of the main reasons many of us visit the backcountry is to see wildlife in their natural environment. But the problem is, most wildlife would prefer to not see us. Use a telephoto lens for photographing animals and binoculars for observing them. A general rule is that if an animal responds to your movements, then you are too close. Teach young children to not harass wildlife and to stay near adults in mountain lion and bear country.

A rare jackalope spotted in White Sands National Monument, New Mexico
(Photo by Mike Frick)

Use Extra Caution During Sensitive Seasons

Winter is a stressful time for many animals because they are conserving a dwindling supply of calories. Fleeing from a skier could spell an animal's death. Spring is a critical time for many species to mate and bear young. Ask a land manager or research the natural history of the place you plan to visit to learn about threatened or endangered species that live there. Try to avoid venturing into these species' habitats during sensitive times.

Control Your Pet

Dogs instinctively want to chase wildlife, so it's best to leave your pet at home. But if you choose to bring Fido, keep him on a leash on the trail and under control in camp. Check with land managers to see if dogs are allowed in the location you plan to visit.

LNT Basics: Respecting Wildlife

- ▲ Keep a clean camp. Avoid dropping food in camp or on the trail.
- ▲ Never give wildlife a handout.
- ▲ Hang or secure all food, garbage, and scented items to avoid habituating area wildlife.
- ▲ Minimize trips to the water source so animals feel free to drink.
- ▲ Observe wildlife from a distance. Use a telephoto lens for photographing animals and binoculars for observing them. If an animal responds to your movements, then you are too close.
- ▲ Use extra caution during sensitive seasons. Ask a land manager or research the natural history of the place you plan to visit to learn about threatened or endangered species that live there.
- ▲ Control your pet. Dogs are often better left home. But if you bring your pet, keep it on a leash on the trail and under control in camp.

Chapter 5

The Wilderness on Foot
LNT GUIDELINES FOR HIKERS, CLIMBERS, AND BACKCOUNTRY SKIERS

hen I backpack through wilderness areas in southern Utah, I always feel a certain kinship with the Ancestral Pueblo people who traveled through the same canyons hundreds of years before me. They, like me, were walkers. They did not have horses or the wheel for locomotion—they relied on their arms and legs to get them everywhere they needed to go.

An intricate system of ancient paths throughout the Southwest's Four Corners region testifies to the long distances the Ancestral Puebloans traveled on foot. Ladders comprised of handholds and footholds carved into sheer rock below the ruins of their cliff dwellings prove they were skilled climbers. And artifacts resembling snowshoes indicate these people kept walking in winter.

Hiking, climbing, snowshoeing, and skiing are quiet and simple forms of foot-propelled travel. Unfortunately, many backcountry pathways are now crowded with hikers, popular cliff faces are crawling with climbers, and once-remote winter wonderlands are congested with backcountry skiers. The growing number of people enjoying these very basic outdoor pursuits causes a variety of environmental complications.

If we are to preserve our wildlands for future generations, it is just as important for a solo hiker to take precautions to minimize his or her impact on the land as it is for a large horsepacking party. What follows is a look at some of the particular environmental and social concerns that come with hiking, climbing, and backcountry skiing, and a guide to specific LNT techniques that will help you minimize your impact.

Hiking: Life in the Trenches

Merely walking through the wilderness seems innocuous enough. However, it is by far the most common mode of recreational travel, and all those little footprints can combine to create a big environmental mess. In fact, increased trail use by hikers has prompted most land managers to cite erosion and plant damage caused by human trampling as the number one trail problem in wilderness areas.

Such destruction is not completely the hikers' fault. Many paths in national parks and Forest Service wilderness areas are old game trails or routes blazed by frontier settlers more than a century ago. These trails are often poorly constructed and placed in less than optimal locations that promote, rather than help prevent, user-caused erosion. In Great Smoky Mountains National Park, for example, most

A badly eroded trail *(Photo by Jeff Marion)*

of the 930 miles of official park trails follow historic wagon roads or old railroad grades that were built for hauling timber.

"The wagon roads vary in design, often crisscrossing streams, ascending ridges, and showing evidence of severe erosion long before their use as trails," noted a 1994 study of park trail conditions by John Wilson and Joseph Seney. Not surprisingly, the study found that a high level of visitor traffic on park trails, combined with poor trail construction, made the environmental condition of these paths, in most cases, downright unsightly. "Trail widening around muddy sections in excess of 12 feet is not uncommon," noted the study.

Minimizing Trail Erosion

In a perfect world, the trail maintenance budget for Great Smoky Mountains National Park and other public lands would be adequate for land managers to reroute poorly located trails and maintain deteriorating paths. However, this is rarely the case because most federal land management agency budgets are of dismal proportions and if any trail maintenance is performed at all, it is done by volunteer groups. Consequently, the best way to keep bad trails from getting worse is for hikers to walk softly and smartly, and, basically, abide by the Leave No Trace principle of "camp and travel on durable surfaces."

What is a durable surface? Is it best to travel on existing trails or hike cross-country? The answer to these questions can vary dramatically depending on your geographic location and the type of area—a crowded state park versus a remote Alaskan wilderness, for example. Just as with choosing a campsite, deciding when and where to leave your bootprints is a judgment call that should be based on your consideration of pertinent environmental factors and minimum-impact hiking techniques.

▲ First, find out about any hiking or trail restrictions that have been imposed by the local land manager. If you are visiting a location where use is high and off-trail trampling is a big problem, such as the White Mountains in New Hampshire or Phoenix Mountain Preserve in Arizona, policies may require you to stay on established trails, and wandering cross-country could be illegal.

▲ In places that receive a fair to heavy amount of use, it is usually best to concentrate impact and stick to designated trails. Traveling cross-country may give you more privacy or improve the aesthetics of your backpacking experience, but where your boots tread, others will surely follow. In some environments, such as a forest understory, it only takes a few people passing on the same route to trample sensitive plants to death and create a discernible path where there once was none.

▲ When hiking on existing trails, make sure you follow the designated main trail and not "volunteer" trails that are often created by people trying to avoid mud or shortcut up switchbacks.

Established hiking trails are usually the paths of least resistance. *(Photo by Robert Kozlow)*

- ▲ Wear gaiters and walk through the mud rather than contributing to the widening of the trail by tiptoeing around the muck in an effort to keep your feet clean.
- ▲ If you will be traveling on fairly flat, dry terrain and your pack is not too heavy, consider wearing lightweight hiking boots instead of the heavy, lug-soled variety. Although studies on how different kinds of hiking boot treads impact trail erosion have been inconclusive, there is no reason to pummel mild terrain with the tread equivalent of a tractor tire.
- ▲ Other ways to minimize trail erosion include walking single file and avoiding locations altogether that you know are especially muddy after a rain or during spring snowmelt.

Cross-country Travel

When you visit remote backcountry areas where established trails are few and far between, and durable surfaces exist for travel routes, hiking cross-country may well be a responsible minimum-impact choice. When you get right down to it, trails themselves are a kind of impact and, on a philosophical level, contradictory to the mandate of the Wilderness Act to keep designated lands free of signs of humans.

Trekking Poles: Pros and Cons

A Few Pointers on Minimizing Impact

You've seen them. Scratches on rocks. Dirt clods. Pockmarks along the trail. The sides of many popular hiking paths look like a car roof after a hailstorm.

These are the residue of trekking poles. Many hikers hate the aesthetic and environmental intrusion caused by the high-tech walking sticks. But other backpackers swear by their poles, saying they couldn't safely complete a wilderness trek without them.

Ground zero of the pole controversy is the Appalachian Trail (AT) where, according to a survey by USGS research biologist Jeff Marion, 90 to 95 percent of through-hikers use trekking poles. "As more people use trekking poles, more people worry about their environmental and social impacts," wrote Marion in *The Register*, an Appalachian Trail newsletter. In the article, Marion said no formal research has been done to evaluate pole concerns but he shared his personal observations on the subject.

"Trailside vegetation can be damaged from the swinging action of trekking poles, particularly from contact with the baskets, which can get caught in low growing plants," noted Marion. He also said AT hikers complained about places where the trail "looked like it had been freshly plowed" from pole tips, and that in these areas soil could become eroded and lose organic litter. The pointed carbide pole tips also leave scratch marks on rock and disturb lichen. And then there's the clinking sound of metal on rock that can get on the nerves of pole-free hikers.

But those poles do come in handy on wet, slippery rocks along the AT. Not to mention in the Grand Canyon and other super-steep hiking locales. Trekking poles offer backpackers stability in treacherous terrain and much-needed support for those with bad knees. And, after all, Marion reasoned that "some amount of resource impact is an inevitable consequence of nearly every form of recreational activity, including hiking without poles."

Marion suggests that LNT-minded hikers use these pole practices to minimize their impact:

▲ Look before you plant. Avoid or minimize damage to vegetation, soils, and rock by paying attention to where your poles are landing.
▲ Use rubber tips as much as possible. (An informal study by Marion showed that rubber tips caused half the soil erosion of metal tips.) Metal, however, is often necessary for safety reasons on steep or wet rock.
▲ Remove baskets unless traveling in snow so vegetation is not disturbed.
▲ Use poles only when you need them. Strap them to your pack on long, flat stretches.

But on a practical level, being able to travel cross-country without scarring the land, and not leaving a path that will invite others to follow behind you, is a very difficult thing to do. Sticking to a designated trail is much easier than constantly weighing the environmental pros and cons that come with choosing a cross-country route.

If you choose to hike cross-country, or find yourself in a situation where you have no other choice, keep in mind the following:

▲ The most durable surfaces for cross-country travel are gravel, sand, slickrock, snow, dry alpine meadows and grasslands, and deep duff beneath a dense forest overstory.

▲ Avoid striking out on a vegetated forest floor or on soggy meadows and grasslands—this terrain is far less resistant to trampling.

▲ Some special types of soils, such as cryptobiotic crusts in desert environments (see Chapter 8, "Special Environments"), should be diligently avoided because a single bootprint lasts for years.

▲ Hiking across a trail-free landscape can be an exhilarating experience, but not if you get lost. Before heading out, make sure you have the proper topographical map for the area and know how to read it.

▲ Never compensate for your lack of orienteering skills by scarring the land to mark your route with tree blazes, cairns, or other signs.

▲ Avoid traversing steep slopes; heel marks gouged into the soil invariably cause erosion.

▲ The best way for a group to minimize the impact of their cross-country travel is to spread out across the landscape rather than walking single file.

Avoiding Conflicts with Other Users

It is important to be realistic about what you can expect when visiting a certain backcountry location. Finding solitude is no longer a given in wilderness areas—especially those that are located within a few hours' drive of major cities. If solitude and/or avoiding horsepacking parties or mountain bike riders is a top priority, research the trail you plan to hike ahead of time and find out from a knowledgeable land manager what kind of traffic the area receives.

▲ In the event you encounter a party of horse riders, the courteous thing to do—because pack animals can be spooked—is to pull off on the downhill side of the trail until the group passes.

▲ If you encounter a mountain biker who does not yield or is in an area off-limits to fat tires, politely inform him or her of the offense; perhaps the behavior is the result of ignorance or can be changed with a little positive peer pressure.

Climbing: Everyone Wants a Piece of the Rock

Steve Matous started climbing back in 1971 when there was no substitute for a mountain. There was no such thing as a climbing gym. Either you hiked 10 miles or more into the wilderness to reach the base of the climb or you stayed home. You had no control over the weather or the condition of the rock. You learned how to

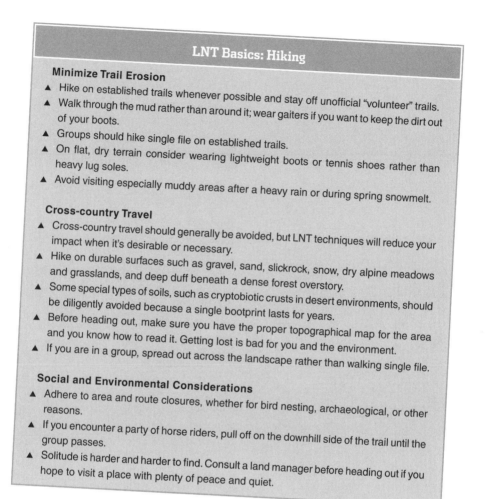

LNT Basics: Hiking

Minimize Trail Erosion

▲ Hike on established trails whenever possible and stay off unofficial "volunteer" trails.

▲ Walk through the mud rather than around it; wear gaiters if you want to keep the dirt out of your boots.

▲ Groups should hike single file on established trails.

▲ On flat, dry terrain consider wearing lightweight boots or tennis shoes rather than heavy lug soles.

▲ Avoid visiting especially muddy areas after a heavy rain or during spring snowmelt.

Cross-country Travel

▲ Cross-country travel should generally be avoided, but LNT techniques will reduce your impact when it's desirable or necessary.

▲ Hike on durable surfaces such as gravel, sand, slickrock, snow, dry alpine meadows and grasslands, and deep duff beneath a dense forest overstory.

▲ Some special types of soils, such as cryptobiotic crusts in desert environments, should be diligently avoided because a single bootprint lasts for years.

▲ Before heading out, make sure you have the proper topographical map for the area and you know how to read it. Getting lost is bad for you and the environment.

▲ If you are in a group, spread out across the landscape rather than walking single file.

Social and Environmental Considerations

▲ Adhere to area and route closures, whether for bird nesting, archaeological, or other reasons.

▲ If you encounter a party of horse riders, pull off on the downhill side of the trail until the group passes.

▲ Solitude is harder and harder to find. Consult a land manager before heading out if you hope to visit a place with plenty of peace and quiet.

climb from mentors who knew the mountain and its many moods. And, in the process, you learned respect for the outdoors.

The popularity and proliferation of climbing gyms over the last two decades has brought many more people to the sport. And a whole new generation of climbers raised in the gym instead of outdoors has changed the dynamics of what used to be a fairly obscure pastime. "If the only relationship they have with climbing is in the gym, then there's a disconnect when they go outdoors," explains Matous. "It's not that people who are used to climbing in the gym are without an environmental ethic. They just don't know what's appropriate in the wilderness and they need to be educated."

Mark Magnuson, a ranger at Grand Teton National Park and Leave No Trace Master is less forgiving. In an LNT newsletter article he said: "Most climbers used

Sport climbing has boomed in popularity over the last decade. *(Photo by Dennis Lewon)*

to come from a tradition of hiking, camping, and outdoorsmanship. Somewhere along the line, the climbing community lost its land ethic."

Although many new climbers who consider themselves environmentally sensitive would likely take issue with Magnuson's assessment, few can dispute the fact that—attitudes aside—just the sheer number of people recently drawn to the sport causes many popular climbing areas to be trashed. A proliferation of unnecessary trails to routes, campfire scars, litter, and toilet paper flowers are among the preventable human impacts frequently encountered in once pristine spots. At the very least, these blemishes take away from the outdoor experience of other users; at the very worst—from a climber's perspective—land managers close areas to climbing in an effort to protect the resource.

Indeed, El Capitan in Yosemite has experienced so much visitation from climbers that the accumulation of human waste in some places on the mountain has created what some rangers describe as "open sewers." To cope with the waste problem, park managers now require climbers on the more popular big walls to pack out their poop. It is one of many new regulations and controversies that have popped up as a result of the hordes of people who are drawn to what was once an obscure sport.

In addition to being a longtime climber, Matous is also the executive director of The Access Fund. The nonprofit organization works to keep climbing areas open and promote environmental conservation of those areas. The Access Fund works in partnership with the Leave No Trace program to educate climbers (both traditional and of the gym variety) about proper wilderness etiquette. "The increased numbers of people enjoying the benefits of climbing make it more important than ever that we protect the vertical resource we depend on," explains Access Fund LNT literature. "Noise, crowding, and poorly planned trails that exacerbate erosion are a few of the indications that we need to step up our efforts to preserve the climbing environment." (For more information on The Access Fund, see the appendix.)

Environmentally responsible climbing boils down to putting the resource first rather than the route. This means you should consider how your behavior in a climbing area—from dropping a cigarette butt to driving a bolt in the rock—impacts the environmental integrity of the landscape. Obviously, there are no such concerns in a climbing gym, but there is also no replacement for the real thing.

Take the Best Approach
Leave No Trace climbing begins with the approach. Instead of making a beeline through the brush to get to the base of the climb, look for an established trail. Concentrating traffic on one primary trail helps protect vegetation in the area and keeps soils from being trampled by a multitude of carelessly created footpaths.

"Many climbers think the only impacts are on the rock but they need to realize the biggest impacts these days are on the ground," Pete Walka, an avid Flagstaff, Arizona, climber, told me. A graduate student at Northern Arizona University's School of Forestry, Walka studies recreation impacts from climbers for his master's thesis. He says the skyrocketing popularity of bouldering has led to many new on-the-ground impacts. "When you throw your crash pad on a bush, it's going to kill it. People should try to keep trampled areas at the base from expanding. Don't throw your gear down at the edge of the area." Walka adds that staging areas in many places resemble the severe environmental degradation of a "blown-out campsite."

If you are setting up camp near the base, try to locate an established site, and follow the minimum-impact guidelines detailed in Chapter 2, "All About Camping," and Chapter 3, "Waste Not, Want Not."

Responsible Waste Disposal

Take extra care in camp and when climbing to pack out all your trash—and that left by others before you. Small pieces of litter, such as cigarette butts or apple cores, add up in popular climbing areas. Plus, food scraps of any kind attract animals and disrupt their natural feeding habits. Consider taking a trash bag with you up the crag to help pick up all the crud that less-conscientious climbers left behind.

Proper disposal of human waste is an increasingly problematic issue as more and more climbers are drawn to rock. One of the contributions The Access Fund most commonly makes to climbing areas is paying for the installation of vault toilets near popular crags. If you are climbing where there is a toilet, use it for all your evacuation needs.

In the absence of a toilet, climbers (like backpackers) usually do not have a lot of good options for LNT-approved poop placement. If you happen to be in a spot where there is a lot of fairly deep organic soil around, you can dig a cat hole; or if you are in a very remote alpine area above tree line, smearing the stuff on a rock may be the way to go. Leaving your waste hidden under a rock is a bad choice because it will decompose slowly and could pollute water sources. Often the best evacuation technique—and the one required in an increasing number of popular climbing areas—is to pack out your poop.

It once was accepted practice for big wall climbers and climbers ascending multiple-day routes to make deposits in paper bags and toss them over the side. However, this is now against land management regulations in many places, including Yosemite and Zion National Parks, and it is an environmentally and socially irresponsible option just about anywhere you toss it. Today the preferred methods for wall climbers who pack it out are disposable bag systems and the poop tube—a homemade PVC pipe contraption that hangs neatly from the bottom of the climber's haul sack (for details on how to build your own, see Chapter 7, "Minimizing Impacts on Waterways").

Considering Others

When climbing, choose a route that will not disturb wildlife or archaeological sites. Pay attention to where birds, especially owls, falcons, eagles, hawks, and other raptors, circle and land on cliff faces and bluffs. If it appears a bird may have a nest near where you are planning to climb, choose another route. Birds are easily stressed by humans approaching their nests, especially during spring and early summer.

In the event that you inadvertently encounter a nest on a climb, never touch it; human contact can cause the adults to abandon the nest and its eggs or young. Land managers in parks and wilderness areas often impose seasonal closures at climbing areas to protect nesting sites. Respect these temporary regulations and find another place to climb.

Likewise, many excellent climbing routes, especially in the Southwest, are located near ancient Native American archaeological sites. Avoid touching or disturbing rock art and ruins, and respect land management restrictions imposed to protect these resources. (For more information on how to minimize impact around archaeological and historical sites, see Chapter 8, "Special Environments.")

Also, be aware of your social impact at climbing areas; for most people, the desired atmosphere at outdoor destinations is often quite different from that typically found at a gym. Loud boom boxes, barking and/or unleashed dogs, and climbers monopolizing routes can ruin the experience of other climbers trying to enjoy the area. In popular climbing areas where you share the spot with others, it is best to leave the boom box and dog at home.

Protecting the Rock

Finally, climbers should do as much as possible to minimize the direct impact their sport has on the rock, without compromising their personal safety. For instance:

Protection. Use removable protection and natural anchors wherever possible; placing bolts and pitons scars the rock and can detract from a climbing area's natural beauty.

Prior to 1970, it was a common practice for climbers to ascend a route by hammering pitons into the rock, which inevitably damaged the resource and caused land managers to close areas to climbers in some popular places. Equipment manufacturers responded to the problem by developing devices known as removable protection—aluminum wedges, cams, and spring-loaded camming devices that can be placed and then removed from a route without damaging the rock. Relying on removable protection to ascend a route, called "clean climbing," has been standard practice among environmentally conscious climbers for nearly three decades and is clearly the best way to "leave no trace" on the rock.

Chalk. Minimize your use of chalk. Like fixed anchors, chalk leaves marks on the rock—albeit less permanent—that others see, and it detracts from the natural character of the landscape. Use a sock or ball to reduce the amount of chalk on

LNT Basics: Climbing

▲ Follow established trails when approaching a route.
▲ When camping at the base of the climb, try to stay at established campsites.
▲ Avoid increasing impacts at the base of climbs and bouldering routes by concentrating people and gear in the middle of a trampled area rather than at the edge of it.
▲ Pack out all trash in camp and on the climbing route (bring a trash bag to pick up litter left by others).

Waste Disposal
▲ Use an outhouse whenever one is available.
▲ Dig a cat hole if there is enough organic soil in the area where you are climbing.
▲ In the absence of an outhouse or diggable soil, pack out your poop in a PVC pipe or other device (never toss it off the mountain).

Social and Environmental Considerations
▲ Adhere to area or route closures, whether for bird nesting, archaeological, or other reasons.
▲ Avoid climbing near bird nests and archaeological sites.
▲ In popular climbing areas where you share the spot with others, it is probably best to leave the boom box and dog at home.

Minimize Impacts on the Rock
▲ Use removable protection and natural anchors wherever possible.
▲ Exercise good judgment when deciding how to get down. Use either an established rappel station or an established descent route (if using the path will not obviously contribute to its deterioration).
▲ Try to use as little chalk as possible.
▲ The process of scrubbing—also known as gardening—should be carried out with great discretion on a new route, and vegetation should be disturbed only for safety reasons rather than aesthetic ones.

your hands. The sock method involves taking an old sock, putting chalk in it and tying it off, and then placing it in your chalk bag. The ball is a commercial version of the sock concept. Either way, you get just a little bit of chalk on your hands, which means less on the rock—and some climbers claim the minimal chalk approach even gives you a better grip. Keep your chalk bag closed when it's not in use.

Scrubbing. Avoid disturbing the rock to make a route more comfortable. The process of scrubbing—also known as gardening—should be carried out with great discretion on a new route, and vegetation should only be disturbed for safety reasons rather than aesthetic ones. Never chip or alter the rock in any way to create better hand- or footholds.

Bolting. Follow the practices established by the agency that oversees the climbing site. You can minimize the visual impact of a bolt by using camouflaged bolt hangers and camouflaged webbing for the rappel anchor, and by placing the bolt in a spot that is not so obvious from the ground.

Descending. Once you have completed the ascent, getting down raises another impact issue—rappelling versus walking off. Good LNT judgment is key here. If hiking down is possible, if the area has an established trail you can use, and if the trail is not suffering from trampling or erosion, walking off may be the best option. However, if you are in a popular area and trampling is a problem (or walking off just is not possible), rappelling will likely be the way to go. Never run rappel ropes around trees. They will be harder to retrieve and pulling them will dig fatal grooves into the trees.

Backcountry Skiing: Protecting the Winter Wonderland

Venturing into the backcountry for a camping trip during the dead of winter, when the ground is covered with deep snow and temperatures dip below zero, used to be the pastime of a few warm-blooded souls. National parks like Yellowstone, with

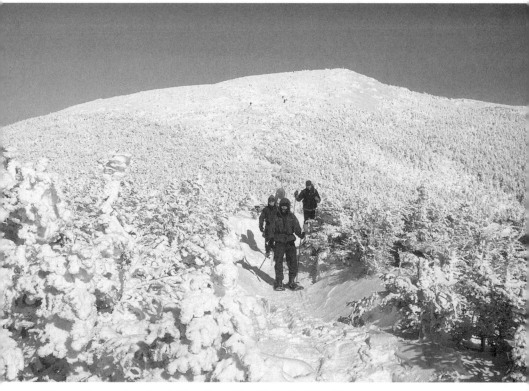

Winter wilderness travelers in New Hampshire *(Photo by Robert Kozlow)*

bumper-to-bumper traffic in the summer, were completely devoid of people. But lately the advent of high-tech, cold-weather gear, along with the increasing number of people who desire to experience wilderness settings in solitude, has made backcountry skiing and winter camping a popular pursuit. In fact, winter sports are among the fastest-growing outdoor pursuits in the United States.

In national parks, for example, winter visitation increased 27 percent in the last decade, while summer visitation increased only 7 percent. The Yellowstone backcountry now gets so many visitors during winter that park managers are considering imposing restrictions to handle human impacts.

The good thing about backcountry skiing and winter camping is that some of the biggest impact problems during other times of year—trampling of trails and campsites—are, essentially, nonexistent when the ground is covered with a thick blanket of snow. However, the potential for stressing wildlife is significantly greater during winter and is the biggest LNT challenge.

Snow Camping

Even though the nights are cold and long, try to resist the urge to have a campfire. During winter, when all downed wood is buried under the snow and the only

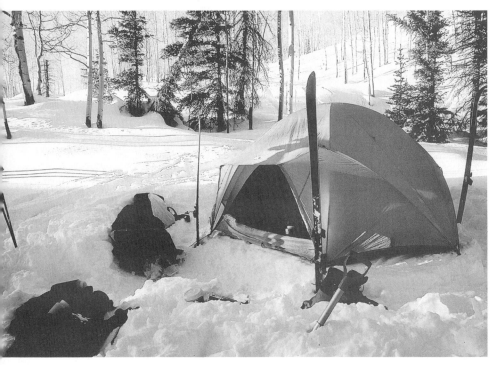

When snow camping, avoid building a fire; use your stove and good clothing for warmth. *(Photo by Chris Gould)*

Winter peak-bagging is increasingly popular in New Hampshire and elsewhere.
(Photo by Robert Kozlow)

available fuel is tree branches, fires are a bad idea. As a "warm-glow" alternative, bring plenty of fuel for your stove and try candle lanterns.

Upon leaving camp, dismantle your snow shelter and fluff up the white stuff so that visitors coming after you can enjoy a natural setting.

Winter Waste Disposal

The best option for waste disposal in snow-covered environs is to pack it out (refer to the methods described in the climbing section of this chapter); burying your poop in the snow is often ineffective, because it may stay frozen until spring and then reappear in full form. When you pee, be sure to do it away from ski trails, and cover up the yellow snow so others do not have to look at it.

Watching Out for Wildlife

In snowy climates, winter is the toughest time of year for mammals that do not hibernate. As food becomes more difficult to find, the animals have less energy, and they must conserve every last ounce to help them find their next meal. When a deer or elk, for example, sees a skier approaching, its natural instinct is to flee, which elevates its heart rate and uses up valuable energy reserves. For a healthy animal during a normal winter, this may not cause serious problems, but if the winter is particularly harsh and the snow is deep, the added stress of humans can be fatal.

When traveling through the backcountry, never approach wildlife, and try to stick to established ski trails so that human activity is contained in a specific area. Although there is plenty of research confirming that humans stress wildlife in winter, no set distance has been established as an adequate buffer zone between you and the animal; several hundred yards should be enough. Also, take extra care to avoid locating your camp where there is animal sign (which is easy to see in the snow) that indicates you are in a spot where wildlife feed, water, or sleep.

LNT Basics: Backcountry Skiing

Watch Out for Wildlife

▲ When traveling through the backcountry, never approach wildlife; try to stick to established ski trails so that human activity is contained in a specific area.

▲ Take extra care to avoid locating your camp where there is animal sign indicating you are in a spot where wildlife feed, water, or sleep.

Waste Disposal

▲ Pack out your poop if you can't dig a cat hole in soil.

▲ When you pee, do it away from trails.

Snow Camping

▲ Resist the urge to have a campfire when deep snow prevents you from reaching downed wood.

▲ Upon leaving camp, dismantle your snow shelter and fluff up the white stuff so that visitors coming after you can enjoy a natural setting.

Chapter 6

Riding Softly in the Saddle
LNT GUIDELINES FOR MOUNTAIN BIKERS AND EQUESTRIANS

sk land managers what is the most common gripe they hear from backcountry users, and the answer probably will be unruly mountain bikers or obnoxious horsepackers. In terms of sheer numbers, because hikers comprise the largest wildland user group, there are likely far more unruly and/or obnoxious hikers in many backcountry areas. But there is something about those horses and bicycles that really gets under people's skin—when they are not the ones sitting in the saddle, of course.

The 1994 survey by John Wilson and Joseph Seney of hiker-biker relations in the popular Rattlesnake National Recreation Area (NRA), located on the outskirts of Missoula, Montana, showed that nearly two-thirds of the hikers found mountain bikes on area trails "objectionable." The two most common reasons given by hikers were "too many bicycles" and "bicycles traveling too fast."

The user-conflict situation for hikers and horsepackers is not much better. In Montana's Bob Marshall Wilderness Complex, for example, horse use increased 20 percent between 1970 and 1983. During that same period, the number of hikers entering the wilderness nearly doubled. The result of this significant increase in wilderness use—albeit primarily from hikers—was a barrage of complaints to land managers about negative impacts of pack stock. Hikers objected to having to walk

The Multiple-Use Solution

The history of the world is rife with turf battles. For as long as anyone can remember, people of different cultures, religions, and agendas have refused to share their territory, preferring to duke it out instead.

Among such ongoing disputes are the conflicts between recreational user groups visiting our nation's public lands. It may seem like a minuscule concern compared to other conflicts raging around the planet, but the inability of different types of people to get along while trying to have fun in the backcountry is the source of major headaches for land managers.

In the late 1980s, hostilities between mountain bikers and hikers in northern California escalated to the point of biker-hiker clashes. Bones were broken and some anti-biking vigilantes booby-trapped trails with fishing line to halt (and injure) speeding members of the knobby-tire set. However, that was about the height of the violence in user conflicts; usually these encounters result in nothing more than heated verbal exchanges and complaints to land managers.

The real danger of ill will between the many different people visiting the backcountry is that it undermines environmental protection of our public lands. While larger threats loom—such as irresponsible logging of national forests and commercial development in and around parks—land managers are distracted by the never-ending conflicts between hikers, horseback riders, and mountain bikers. But if these three substantial user groups were to comprise a unified front, they would be a conservation force to be reckoned with—possibly large enough to shape management decisions and protect our public lands from being eaten away by consumptive uses such as logging, mining, grazing, and development.

So why don't nonmotorized recreationists get along in the backcountry? Part of the problem lies in the same reason people are rude to each other on the New York City subway—it is too crowded. This is not the case everywhere, but the majority of people go to the same places, to the most accessible Forest Service lands and the most popular national parks. Most of the 830 million recreation visits to national forest lands in 2001 occurred in a limited number of wilderness areas and other popular destinations that are within a few hours drive of metropolitan areas.

"Trails in or near cities tend to be crowded, and crowded trails breed user conflict," says Tim Blumenthal, executive director of the International Mountain Biking Association. "The key factor is more people. There is a gap between expectations and reality. The farther you are from a population center, the more likely it is that you expect solitude. And as we all know, solitude is getting tougher to find."

Considering our differences, and the inevitable prospect that recreational use of public lands will continue to increase, can we nonmotorized folks ever expect to all get along? The answer to this dilemma in most places across the country is that we have no choice. At best, the amount of public lands available for recreational pursuits will stay generally the same, which means that the increased number of hikers, mountain bikers, and horseback riders will vie for finite trail space, and the potential for user conflicts will increase proportionately.

Sometimes land managers consider segregating trail users—putting, for example, horseback riders on one path and directing hikers to another route—but spreading human impact over a larger region makes this a counterproductive move from an environmental standpoint. Closing trails to certain users, such as mountain bikers, is often counterproductive as well, because it denies access to a large and growing trail-constituency group.

In most cases, the best solution is to manage trails as "multiple use" (open to hikers, horse riders, and mountain bikers in non-wilderness areas, and open to hikers and horse riders in wilderness areas), and to rely on users to educate one another on the principles of Leave No Trace and basic manners.

Whether it is deciding to split a large—and potentially loud—party into smaller camping groups or yielding right-of-way on the trail, practicing good wilderness manners boils down to being considerate and keeping in mind the big conservation picture. Most of the nation's newest long-distance paths, such as the American Discovery Trail, the Continental Divide Trail, and the Arizona Trail, are designed, at least in part, to be shared by hikers, horseback riders, and mountain bikers.

The multiple-use approach is working. Trail access is easier to obtain from land managers when there is a broad base of user support, and, likewise, when a large community of trail users exists to help maintain and protect the nonmotorized path when it is completed. Plus, from a conservation standpoint, a nonmotorized trail constituency that is unified is far more effective in fighting larger, more political environmental threats such as proposals to allow clear-cutting near trails, or strip mining, or opening the path to off-road vehicles. If backcountry recreationists are going to engage in a turf war, it might as well be a battle worth fighting.

through too much horse crap, and complained of environmental destruction to trails, campsites, and riparian areas caused by the proliferation of the large beasts.

As in almost all research conducted on user conflicts, both the Rattlesnake NRA and Bob Marshall Wilderness studies showed that the "conflict relationship" between the differing parties was "asymmetrical." That is, while the hikers were generally annoyed by the mountain bikers and horsepackers, only a few bikers or equestrians reported having their visitor experience negatively impacted by hikers.

Whether mountain bikes or horses actually cause more environmental damage to a wildland destination than hikers varies dramatically from place to place, depending on the type of terrain and behavior of the various user groups. There is no denying, however, that fat tire tracks and hoofprints leave a very recognizable mark on the land—especially if it is in a place that receives more than its fair share of human visitors.

History has borne out that when user conflicts and/or environmental impacts become too great in a particular backcountry area, land managers often close trails to mountain bikers and pack stock. Regardless of whether this is deserved in any particular situation is beside the point. The real prospect that tracts of public land can be made off-limits to biking or horseback riding even for perceived environmental impacts should be motivation enough to adopt Leave No Trace practices. But, even more important, it is the responsibility of all users—including mountain bikers and equestrians—to do their share in preserving the landscape and sense of solitude that make wildlands so special. To that end, here are some specific LNT guidelines and minimum-impact techniques for you to ride by.

Mountain Biking: As the Fat Tire Turns

Back in 1964 when Congress passed the Wilderness Act, the only two modes of nonmotorized travel on public lands was by foot or horse. Few could have anticipated that twenty years later millions of people would be vying for space on trails atop all-terrain knobby-tire bicycles. Ownership of mountain bikes in the United States has exploded over the last several decades from essentially zero in the late 1970s, when the fat tire machine was invented, to some 26 million today. Many of these bike owners stick to city sidewalks and rural roads, but millions are dedicated backcountry trail riders as well. The rapid onslaught of this new user group has, perhaps, impacted the experiences of all wildland recreationists more than any other recent public lands development.

Learning Social Graces

Impact problems associated with mountain biking in the backcountry are as much—or more—social as environmental. Hikers and horse riders do not like the feeling of almost being mowed down by a group of speeding mountain bikers. Even when there are no mountain bikers in sight, their tracks on the trail are easily recognizable and, for many other users, instantly despicable. For land managers, there is often little more irritating than seeing the telltale fat tire tracks on wilderness trails where mountain bikes are off-limits.

"We have to overcome a stereotype," says International Mountain Biking Association (IMBA) executive director Tim Blumenthal about mountain biking's reputation as an environmentally insensitive gonzo sport. "It is not just the gonzo riders anymore; a broad range of people are getting into off-road mountain biking these days." However, Blumenthal also points out that a single gonzo rider blasting past forty people on a trail over the course of a day can do a lot to perpetuate mountain biking's bad-boy image. "A mountain biker breaking the rules of the trail is very noticeable," he notes. "But if a hiker were to take off cross-country up a hill rather than going up the switchbacks, few other people would probably see it."

Formed in 1988 in response to the increasing number of trails that were being closed to fat tires, the IMBA works with land managers and the public to protect public land access for mountain bikes, and to teach this new user group some manners. Although the IMBA counts many success stories in securing access for mountain bikers, Blumenthal acknowledges that several big problems still exist for the future of fat-tire trail travel. "We have not been around long enough or presented ourselves well enough to command widespread respect." He continues, "We have to figure a way to corral unruly riders who ignore trail signs and hammer on busy routes."

Mountain biking in Box Canyon, Arizona *(Photo by Mike Frick)*

Blumenthal maintains that mountain biking is no more damaging to trails and the environment than foot traffic. A variety of studies on the subject have concluded as much, including the 1994 Wilson-Seney report that evaluated mountain trail erosion in Montana. This particular study found that horse traffic had the greatest potential for causing erosion, followed by hiking traffic, with the fat tire stirring up the least amount of trail soil. However, the report also noted that the findings of the study were "complicated and difficult to decipher."

While research on whether mountain-bike use negatively impacts the environment has been inconclusive, there is no shortage of data documenting how much most hikers dislike sharing the trail with mountain bikers. The survey of hiker-biker relations in Montana's Rattlesnake National Recreation Area that showed nearly two-thirds of the hikers found mountain bikes on area trails "objectionable" also found that, while both hikers and bikers expressed a strong degree of attachment to the area, "bicyclists reported significantly less focus on the setting than the other groups."

But regardless of how they are interpreted, such findings are no license for mountain bikers to be any less conscientious about minimizing their environmental impact. "Tracks in the mud are easy to trace back to bicycles," notes Blumenthal. "Heavy use is going to impact trails no matter what—whether it is coming from bikes or hikers or horses. But mountain bikers have a special responsibility to minimize their impact. And the IMBA is adamant about riders staying on the trail."

Salvation through Soft Cycling

The IMBA and other environmentally conscious mountain biking groups encourage a kind of non-gonzo approach to riding known as "soft cycling." (For more information on the IMBA, see the appendix.) Among the key commandments of this politically correct form of pedaling are:

▲ Stay off muddy trails.

▲ Avoid heavy braking and skidding to protect trail surfaces.

▲ Walk your bike over a trail obstruction rather than cutting a "line" around it.

▲ Stay on switchbacks.

▲ Ride single file and in small groups.

▲ Slow down—especially around other trail users.

The IMBA has incorporated this general "soft cycling" philosophy into its more specific "Rules of the Trail." Like the seven principles of the Leave No Trace program, these six rules are heavily promoted by the IMBA and various mountain bike manufacturers who print the guidelines on water bottles and product hangtags. The six IMBA rules to ride by are:

1. **Ride on open trails only.** Respect trail and road closures; avoid possible trespass on private land. Federal and state wilderness areas are closed to cycling.

2. **Leave no trace.** Be sensitive to the dirt beneath you. Even on open trails, do not ride under conditions in which you will leave evidence of your passing, such as on damp or muddy soils shortly after a rain. This also means staying on the trail and not creating any new ones. Pack out what you pack in. Dispose of human waste properly.

3. **Control your bicycle.** Inattention for even a second can cause problems. Obey all speed laws.

4. **Always yield the trail.** Make known your approach well in advance. Show your respect when passing others by slowing to a walk or even stopping. Anticipate that other trail users may be around corners or in blind spots.

5. **Never scare animals.** All animals are startled by an unannounced approach. Give animals extra room and time to adjust to you. In passing, use special care and follow directions of horseback riders (ask if uncertain).

6. **Plan ahead.** Know your equipment, your ability, and the area in which you are riding—and prepare accordingly. Carry tools and repair supplies (spare tube, patches, pump) to keep your bike in working order. A well-executed trip is a satisfaction to you and not a burden or offense to others.

When it comes to minimizing fat tire impacts and improving the image of mountain biking, Blumenthal points out that it is not just about what you do when you are riding. "We encourage mountain bikers to join a local club, get involved in volunteer trail work, and participate in National Trails Day (held every June)," he says.

Horsepacking: The Ultimate Challenge

Use of pack stock in the backcountry varies significantly with geographic region—in many places in the West it is dominated by organized outfitters leading hunting trips; in some locations it is mostly practiced by individuals who live nearby in a rural area; and in other places, vacationing families rent the horses from concessionaires. But no matter where the domestic animals come from, there is no denying that widespread use of pack stock in the backcountry can result in very noticeable environmental changes to the landscape and negatively influence the experience of other visitors.

Of all nonmotorized modes of travel in the backcountry, horsepacking has the greatest potential for environmental damage. Numerous studies have documented the substantial erosion to trails and destruction to campsites caused by pack stock. On the other hand, Virgil Mink, a recreation wilderness manager with the Tonopah National Forest in Nevada and self-proclaimed "guru" of Leave No Trace horsepacking, maintains that he can take pack stock into the backcountry and create no more impact than a party of hikers.

"Traveling with horses can have a high impact on the land, but the challenges in reducing that impact are not insurmountable," says Mink. Compared to

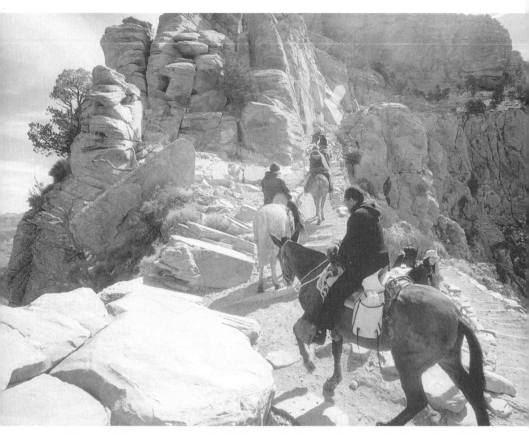

A hiker yields to a mule train on the Bright Angel Trail, Grand Canyon. *(Photo by Mike Frick)*

backpacking, implementing Leave No Trace practices when horsepacking poses some unique and difficult challenges. First, there is the sheer weight of the animal; 1500 pounds bearing down on four hooves has the potential to inflict significant trampling damage on soil and vegetation. Second, horses poop a lot and they do not bury it in cat holes. Aside from this waste being an aesthetic problem for other backcountry users who do not like to step in it, horse manure often contains seeds that introduce ecologically damaging weed species to the environment. And then there is the fact that pack stock like to graze, which defoliates vegetation, and the animals have to be confined at camp, which can cause a mess.

For all these reasons, there is a growing trend among land managers to limit or ban horses in wilderness areas. According to a 1993 Forest Service study of pack stock use, 6 of 308 wilderness areas (2 percent) in 1980 prohibited horsepacking; by 1990 stock use was prohibited in 58 of 423 wilderness areas (14 percent). Although the number of designated wilderness areas across the United States increased, the number of these federal preserves that are open to horsepacking declined.

Mink took on the cause of promoting and developing minimum-impact horsepacking techniques some ten years ago when he was a Forest Service volunteer. "I am a longtime horsepacker," he says, "and I could see the impact that pack stock were having on the environment, and that land managers were going to ban horses from more and more wilderness areas if things did not change."

Mink was not the only one concerned. The Backcountry Horsemen of America, a national equestrian organization with a broad membership (see the appendix), jumped on the minimum-impact bandwagon and began promoting to its members an environmentally sensitive approach to horsepacking. The Leave No Trace staff at NOLS developed an LNT "Master Educator" course designed to teach minimum-impact horsepacking techniques. They also produced an LNT *Backcountry Horse Use* booklet that is distributed to the public by land managers.

Today, the notion of minimizing impact when horsepacking is no longer a novel concept; in fact, various riding clubs around the country pride themselves on their environmental ethics and LNT practices. "The Backcountry Horsemen have jumped on the LNT bandwagon perhaps more than any other user group," notes NOLS Leave No Trace program coordinator Michael Cheek. "They've taken the initiative and directed funds to get LNT Master Educators trained in nearly all their chapters."

"I know in my district it has made a difference," adds Mink. "People who have been gone two years and recently came back to this area say the forest looks better—they do not see the horse impacts like they used to."

All of the seven basic principles of the Leave No Trace program apply to horsepacking, but a host of specific practices are vital to meeting the impact challenges inherent with pack stock. According to Mink, "The main thing is planning." This means finding out ahead of time from the land manager what horse restrictions are in place in the area you will be visiting, and packing as lightly and as smartly as possible. Following is a rundown of some of the key principles of LNT horsepacking.

Learning to Pack Lightly

Traveling light reduces the number of pack animals you need to bring into the backcountry, which is key to minimizing impact.

- ▲ Rather than heavy canvas tents, bring lightweight nylon shelters.
- ▲ Opt for sleeping bags instead of cots.
- ▲ Try using a compact, gas-fueled camp stove instead of cooking over a fire with a big Dutch oven.
- ▲ Pack freeze-dried and dehydrated meals in reusable plastic bags rather than throwing a bunch of canned goods and glass containers in your saddlebags. Mink even encourages people to put their libations in a lightweight flask instead of hauling the whole bottle.

Using Weed-free Feed

It is estimated that invasive weeds spread at a rate of 4600 acres per day on federal lands—a problem that is largely due to seeds transmitted by pack animals.

- ▲ To help stem the spread of noxious weeds in wildlands and to reduce grazing damage to vegetation, bring supplemental feed for your animals that is "certified weed-free."
- ▲ Begin feeding your stock the certified weed-free grub two days before entering the backcountry to prevent the possibility of any noxious seeds being transported through the animals' manure. (Land managers require certified weed-free feed in some wilderness areas.)
- ▲ When in camp, it is also a good idea to feed your stock using a nosebag or manti. This helps the horse eat every last bite of its weed-free dinner and prevents the animal from roughing up the dirt to munch its meal off the ground.

Minimizing Trampling

Because of the inevitable trampling that results from horse travel, it is especially important for pack stock users to stick to designated trails. Other methods for reducing trampling include:

- ▲ Avoid riding on trails during times of the year when much of the path will be muddy. And if you come upon a muddy patch, try to get your horse to go through the middle of it rather than around the muck, which further widens and erodes the trail.

This trail has been heavily trampled by horses. *(Photo by David Cole)*

▲ If you know you will be traveling on fairly even terrain, consider outfitting your horse with flat, plate-style shoes before leaving home. Shoes with heel and toe caulks give horses better traction on steep, rocky, or icy slopes, but they also increase the potential for trail erosion.

▲ If you find it necessary to travel cross-country with your stock, make sure it is on a durable surface, such as dry grassland, and allow your animals to travel abreast to spread impact from trampling rather than keeping them single file.

Resting Carefully

The challenge of minimizing your impact during a horsepacking trip never stops, even when you and your horses take a break. A variety of negative environmental and social impacts can occur in the span of just five minutes.

▲ When taking breaks, move your animals off the trail so others can get by.

▲ Hobble your horses rather than tying them to trees even if it is for just five minutes; a horse tied to a tree trunk can break branches and permanently damage bark and roots.

▲ When watering your horses, keep the animals away from wet, marshy springs, streambanks, and the soggy edges of ponds and lakes. These areas are especially susceptible to trampling, erosion, and pollution. Try to let your animals drink from an established ford or find a low, rocky spot that is less susceptible to trampling. It is also helpful to bring a bucket for watering horses; just fill it up anywhere and let your stock drink 200 feet away from the water source.

▲ Before leaving the resting spot, scatter any horse droppings with a shovel or a swift kick of your boot.

The LNT Horse Camp

Choosing a campsite and a method for restraining horses in camp are easily the most important minimum-impact decisions a horsepacker will make. Because confined animals can significantly scar an otherwise undisturbed backcountry location, it is best to set up camp at an established site—preferably one that is officially or unofficially designated for pack stock use, what Mink calls a "sacrifice site." Consult with the local land manager before your trip to find out where the best pack stock campsites are located.

When it comes to confining your stock, avoid tying them to trees. This longtime practice damages root systems and bark and has killed trees in backcountry areas heavily used by pack stock. Tying horses in this manner also damages the soil

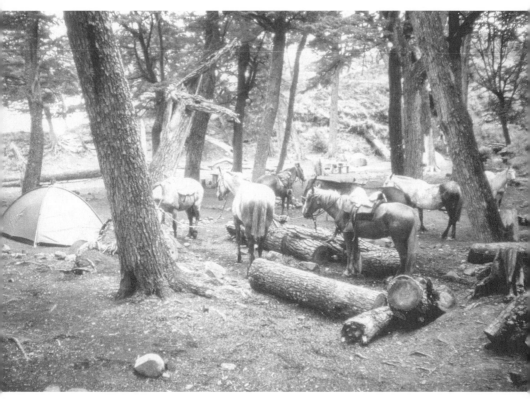

A severely impacted horsepacker camp *(Photo by Jeff Marion)*

around the tree, creating a telltale "doughnut" pounded into the earth by the restless animal. Two effective ways to confine stock and minimize environmental impacts are:

Electric fencing. The personal preference of Mink, this restraining method uses portable electric fencing to create a temporary corral. The fencing is lightweight, powered by flashlight-size batteries, and very effective for pack stock that have been trained to respect it.

The highline. This method involves placing the horses in between two trees where there is little likelihood of trampling damage. To erect a highline, find an area around camp with dry, hardened ground, and stretch a rope at a height a little above the horses' heads between two live trees that are at least 8 inches in diameter. To prevent the rope from girdling the trees, use adjustable nylon "tree saver" straps; gunnysacks come in handy for additional bark padding if needed. Tie the animals' lead ropes at intervals along the highline so that they are away from tree trunks and unable to slide along the line. Make sure each lead rope is long enough to allow the horse some movement, but not so long that it could wrap around the animal's neck or leg. Although the highline is the most common LNT method for restraining horses—and is much better than tying them to trees—it is harder on the environment than electric fencing. Trampling impacts caused by highlining have led some wilderness areas to ban the practice, while others now have designated highline zones.

Regardless of which method you choose for confining your animals, keep them in that location for only one night to reduce trampling and grazing impacts, and be sure to scatter their turd piles when breaking camp.

As for the humans in camp, follow the minimum-impact procedures detailed in Chapters 2 and 3: restrict the use of campfires, properly dispose of human waste, and pack out all garbage. One advantage of horsepacking is it allows people to

Tree saver straps used in a highline

Highline

travel with various items that aid efforts to minimize impact, such as fire pans, bear-proof food boxes, and portable latrines. And remember to respect the desires of others within hearing range, who likely came to the wilderness in search of peace and quiet.

Mink concedes that even though Leave No Trace practices are catching on with individual horsepackers, many outfitters using pack stock are sticking to the old ways. "They have people who pay money with the expectation that they are going to camp like they have seen on the cowboy shows on TV," he says. "Those people want the big, walled canvas tents, the cots, and lots of Dutch oven cooking." Like most wilderness area land managers in the West, Mink attempts to confine the consequences of these outfitter groups by requiring them to camp at designated group sites.

However, the horsepacking "guru" recently came up with another innovative way to keep stock users happy while significantly minimizing their impact. "I have a special trailhead I like to show off," he said. "It has corrals, and I encourage people to camp there and go into the wilderness for day rides. Groups really like it; it has become a preferred spot for horsepackers because they have everything they need there."

Another Option

Over the last decade, llamas have increased in popularity as an alternative to horse-packing. Research biologist Jeff Marion—who's made a career out of researching recreation impacts—owns five llamas to facilitate his family's wilderness excursions.

"They don't carry as much as horses (about 60–80 pounds)," notes Marion. "But they have soft feet, and unless it's really wet, you can't even see their footprints on the trails."

Several studies conclusively proved that llamas are an easier and more effective Leave No Trace option than horses and mules. In addition to having dainty feet (no hooves) that cause less trampling than a hiking boot, llamas poop odorless, seed-free pellets similar to elk poo. Llamas are also from the camel family, which means they absorb most of their necessary fluid from the food they eat and there-fore don't damage streambeds to rehydrate.

LNT Basics: Horsepacking

Packing Light

▲ Use modern camping equipment, including lightweight tents, sleeping bags, and stoves.
▲ Pack freeze-dried and dehydrated meals in reusable plastic bags rather than food in heavy cans and glass containers.

Using Weed-Free Feed

▲ Feed your pack stock certified "weed-free" feed, both in camp and before leaving on your trip.

Minimize Trampling

▲ Avoid riding on trails during times of year when you know much of the path will be muddy.
▲ If you come upon a muddy patch, try to get your horse to go through the middle of it rather than around the muck.
▲ When travel will be across fairly even terrain, consider outfitting your horse with flat, plate-style shoes before leaving home.
▲ During rest breaks, hobble your horses rather than tying them to trees.
▲ When watering your horses, keep the animals away from wet, marshy springs, streambanks, and the soggy edges of ponds and lakes. Try to let your animals drink from an established ford or find a low, rocky spot that is less susceptible to trampling.

The Horse Camp

▲ Minimize your impact when camping by choosing the most durable site. Camp at a site designated for pack stock whenever possible.
▲ Confine your horses in electric fencing or with a highline.
▲ Scatter horse droppings when vacating the site.
▲ Stay at a site for only one night, and then move on.

Chapter 7

Minimizing Impacts on Waterways

LNT GUIDELINES FOR SEA KAYAKERS, CANOEISTS, AND RAFTERS

ecause most of our planet is water, it would seem as though there is more than enough room for all boaters to roam without bumping into each other or negatively impacting the environment. But most paddlers travel on a very small percentage of the earth's wet stuff, typically hugging popular wilderness coastlines and floating the precious few undammed stretches of scenic rivers. Consequently, the concentration of users in places such as coastal barrier islands, canyon river corridors, and lakeshore campsites offers quite a challenge when it comes to Leave No Trace practices.

To further complicate matters, backcountry paddling—whether it is kayaking, canoeing, or rafting—lends itself to traveling in groups and bringing lots of stuff. This need not be inherently damaging to the environment, especially if some of that stuff includes LNT tools such as a fire pan and a portable potty, but such waterborne group pursuits require special minimum-impact considerations on the part of the user.

On the plus side, nonmotorized water travel does not have the same kind of user conflicts that currently rage among ground-based wilderness users. In most places, kayakers, canoeists, and even large parties of rafters seem to get along swimmingly. The key is for these different types of paddlers to travel and camp the LNT way so that heavily visited destinations will continue to be enjoyable. After all, nothing sinks a great float trip faster than lots of litter along a riverbank or human waste washing up onshore.

Sea Kayaking: Paddling Softly in Coastal Environments

Sea kayaking grew rapidly in popularity over the last decade and is having a significant impact on fragile island environments on both the Atlantic and Pacific Coasts, from Maine to Baja. "We are overwhelmed with recreational use," says Sid Quarrier, a volunteer for the Maine Island Trail Association (MITA). "Even though most kayakers try to act in an environmentally responsible manner, the islands are just being taxed through sheer visitor numbers."

The Maine Island Trail is a water route that strings together some eighty designated islands (out of three thousand) along 350 miles of coastline. Although about half of the islands are open to the general public because they are state-owned, the balance is privately owned and open only to MITA members. Most of the islands on the trail are small—about an acre—and uninhabited. The isolated environments and wildlife populations on these islands are particularly fragile, and MITA devotes much of its staff and volunteer time to educating trail users on how to minimize their impact. MITA enlists volunteers who monitor specific islands and visit campsites to talk to paddlers about LNT practices. MITA also publishes a guidebook, half of which is devoted to explaining how to minimize environmental impacts when visiting the islands.

Making Camp

Coastal environments vary greatly depending on where you are on the planet. The forested shores of Alaska, for example, are a far cry from the desert beaches of Baja. Nevertheless, all coastlines have one thing in common: an intertidal zone—a zone that is the most resistant of all natural surfaces to human impact.

In some cases, steep cliffs or wildlife activity make the intertidal zone inaccessible. But whenever possible, conduct all your activities—camping, fire building, hiking, and sanitation—in this zone. In addition, adherence to the following guidelines will help minimize your impact while on a sea kayaking trip:

- ▲ When transferring between land and water, launch and land your vessel on sandy beaches or sloping rock ledges. Scrambling over dirt banks and shrubby ledges promotes erosion that will continue long after you have pushed off.
- ▲ On the shoreline, choose an established campsite in the intertidal zone if such an option is available.
- ▲ Make sure your campsite is above the daily high-tide line, so you don't get

The author and her son Austin kayaking on Lake Powell, Utah *(Photo by Mike Frick)*

washed away, but preferably below the monthly high tide mark (tides are highest during the periods of a new moon and full moon).

⚠ When hiking outside the intertidal zone, stick to durable surfaces such as rocks or an established trail.

⚠ Fragile soils and lack of wood, combined with high visitor use, mean campfires are generally bad news on islands and should be avoided. Do your cooking and hand warming on a camp stove. It may be appropriate to build a fire on a coastal beach, below high tide, if there is plenty of driftwood available and fires are permitted.

Waste Disposal

In coastal environments that are not heavily used by humans, the oceans can act as a natural wastewater treatment system, making "going to the bathroom" quite simple.

As to urination, do it anywhere below the high-tide line and away from tidal pools and other people.

Solid waste management requires a little more discretion. It is illegal to discharge human waste into U.S. waters. If conditions permit, bury your waste, cathole style (see Chapter 3, "Waste Not, Want Not") just above the high-tide line where moist coastal soils will speed decomposition.

Dealing with solid waste on islands with a high volume of visitors, however, is a different story—and an environmental challenge with which MITA is all too familiar. The LNT guidelines set out by MITA can apply to most coastal island environments in North America: pack out all poop. Soil on the islands is shallow and fragile. "One footprint on a lichen bed could last ten years," says Quarrier. Plus, in a space of just one acre, there is not much room for cat holes when people are camping on the islands every night during prime seasons. If you camp on an island anywhere in the Lower 48, chances are you should pack out your poop. In addition to MITA, land managers also require paddlers to pack it out from Utah's Lake Powell, California's Point Reyes National Seashore, and Powell Reservoir in Wisconsin's Apostle Islands. Some of the preferred packing methods used by veteran paddlers follow.

The poop tube. A common item among big-wall climbers, the poop tube works just as well for packing out waste on kayak trips. The tube is a homemade contraption composed of PVC pipe parts that can be purchased at most hardware stores.

- ▲ The PVC pipe should be about 4 inches in diameter and cut to size anywhere from 12 to 25 inches in length (depending on your personal habits and how long you are going to be out there). One end should be threaded, or get a threaded fitting.
- ▲ Glue a cap on one end, using cement recommended for PVC. Glue a threaded fitting on the other end if the pipe itself is not threaded. Get a plug for the end that screws into the pipe threads.
- ▲ Using duct tape and some nylon cord, fashion a loop through the top of the plug and attach it to the pipe. This helps prevent the plug from getting lost and gives you a means for tying the tube to a secure spot.
- ▲ Do your pooping in brown paper bags, toss in a little kitty litter for odor control, and stuff the bags in the tube for safekeeping. At the end of your trip, dispose of the tube contents in a vault toilet or at an RV dump station.

A one-gallon, plastic, resealable container. Use it with a little seawater in it.
A waterproof ammo canister. Line it with a garbage bag.
A biodegradable bag. Carry kitty litter, sand, or leaves in another container.
A bucket with a tight-fitting lid. Use for groups.
An ample-size, resealable, plastic container. One veteran MITA member prefers to deposit her waste on a turfy spot where there are plenty of leaves, sand, or loose soil. She rolls the poop in the substrate and scoops it up with toilet paper or a baggie over the hand, then transfers the stuff to the container. She rinses the hand baggie in saltwater for reuse. She finds her system to be an innocuous approach to packing it out because the poop is well hidden by the leaves and dirt.

There are many other ways to pack it out, and it seems sea kayakers, more than any other recreational group, have a knack for coming up with innovative techniques for transporting their poop. Just keep in mind that it is illegal to dispose of human waste in a dumpster or any trash facility that is not ultimately headed for a sewage treatment plant.

Protecting Wildlife

A major environmental concern for sea kayakers is their impact on wildlife. Although paddling may seem less intrusive than boats with noisy outboard motors, the mere presence of humans is often perceived as a threat by coastal wildlife. Kayakers on the Maine Island Trail, for example, share the territory with populations of seals, sea lions, eagles, and various seabirds, including murres, puffins, and cormorants.

Many islands with nesting populations of these species are closed to camping during sensitive periods. Paddlers are asked to avoid seabird nesting sites from early April through mid-August, and to steer clear of seal populations from mid-May through mid-June, when the animals bear their young. Intrusion into nesting or breeding areas during these times can be devastating to wildlife.

For instance, seals and sea lions haul out on land to form colonies where they give birth and nurse their young. Just one kayak venturing too close to a haul-out site can start a panicked stampede, causing pups to be crushed to death as the adults rush to the water for safety. Even if there are only a few adult seals onshore, the approach of a kayak can cause a mother and her pup to run for the water. In the state of panic, there is a good chance the pup will be separated from its mother, a circumstance that could lead to its eventual death.

Respect all posted wildlife restrictions when paddling in coastal areas, and be especially cautious during spring and summer months. If you see a seal raise its head to look at you, then you are too close. A general rule for most marine wildlife species is to maintain a buffer of at least 100 yards no matter what time of year you are on the water. Invest in good binoculars and a telephoto lens for your camera so that you can view and photograph wildlife species without inadvertently harassing them.

Canoeing and Rafting: Rowing Your Boat Gently

Rafting and canoeing on backcountry rivers are also popular modes of wilderness travel. Of course, people have been using America's waterways to get around for thousands of years, and before the advent of pavement, river corridors were our nation's primary transportation routes.

Because of their utilitarian role, most rivers in the United States have been developed and no longer resemble the pristine riparian environments of several centuries ago. In fact, of the 3 million miles of rivers and streams in the United States, only 0.4 percent are protected as wilderness waterways under the National Wild and Scenic Rivers System. It is this tiny fraction of wilderness rivers that most paddlers want to visit.

The fact that river travelers all float down the same corridors offers advantages and disadvantages from an LNT perspective. The use is inevitably concentrated, so—unlike popular backpacking destinations where hikers roam everywhere—environmental destruction on rivers is generally contained. But large groups of people boating in the same area creates social and environmental challenges, especially when it comes to managing human waste, controlling litter, and minimizing the impact of camping.

These days, canoeing and rafting on popular rivers often comes with plenty of land management regulations. It may seem like a hassle to follow all the minimum-impact procedures, but one need only look at the tidy condition of the Colorado River through the Grand Canyon to see that it is worth it.

An established campsite in the Boundary Waters Wilderness *(Photo by Jeff Marion)*

Making Camp

It is a common management policy on popular rivers to require visitors to camp at designated sites. The objective, of course, is to concentrate use—which is a good idea regardless of whether the land manager requires you to do so.

If you happen to be traveling on a more remote river and cannot find a well-established site, set up camp within the floodplain on beaches or gravel bars. However, if you are traveling during a period of heavy rain or snowmelt and know the water level could rise suddenly and significantly, choose a campsite on a durable surface well above the river.

Maybe because canoes and especially rafts have the capacity for carrying lots of stuff, the potential for people on river trips to accidentally litter is high. Try to repackage foods before a trip to reduce your littering potential. Once in camp, consider laying down a tarp as a "kitchen floor" to catch debris that might otherwise get buried in the sand.

Vegetation in riparian environments is sensitive, and seedlings usually do not stand a chance in and around popular riverside campsites. When in camp, try to conduct as much of your activity as possible below the river's floodplain or in heavily used areas.

Campfires are a problem in river environments primarily because of the lack of wood at established campsites. If you want to have a fire, bring in your own wood or pick up driftwood over the course of the day's paddle. Use a fire pan, and locate the fire on a beach or gravel bar (see Chapter 2 for more on fire-building practices). Many land managers require use of a fire pan and ask that all ashes and charcoal be packed out.

Waste Disposal

If you happen to be on a remote river where you can dig a cat hole at least 200 feet from shore, go ahead and bury your waste. But because of the popularity of many waterways—and the fact that numerous western rivers pass through narrow, slickrock canyons—it has become standard procedure (and often land management policy) for most boaters to pack out their waste. Fortunately, rafts and canoes have a large carrying capacity and are ideally suited for hauling portable toilets to pack out the group poop.

Sanitary conditions on the Colorado River in the Grand Canyon got pretty bad before rafting outfitters came around to wholeheartedly supporting the "pack it out" guideline. In a 1972 poll of Grand Canyon river runners, "Use and Quality of Wildland Water," more than half of those surveyed said they had contracted some form of gastrointestinal illness on the job. Too many people were leaving behind too much poop.

"We were always digging up other people's dump sites, and toilet paper was everywhere," recalls longtime river rat and former Grand Canyon National Park

Slickrock is a good surface on which to cook and unload gear. *(Photo by Annette McGivney)*

wilderness supervisor Kim Crumbo. Crumbo worked as a guide in the canyon in the early '70s when most folks in the rafting community came to agree there was only one option—aside from severely restricting the number of people on the river—and that was to pack out human waste.

In 1979, when Crumbo joined the Grand Canyon National Park staff, it had become Park Service policy and standard outfitter procedure to pack out all poop on river trips. Old ammo "rocket" boxes were used as receptacles, often equipped with a removable toilet seat for customer comfort. The honor of slop duty usually went to the most junior guide on the trip. Today, the number of people rafting through the canyon hits 23,000 annually, but the river environment is far cleaner than it was back in the early '70s—and the guides are not getting sick.

Since the poop-packing rule was first implemented in the Grand Canyon in the late 1970s, a host of companies have developed a variety of portable potties designed primarily for river travel. A summary of what is available is found in *How to Shit in the Woods*, by Kathleen Meyer. Here are some of the highlights from Meyer's plethora of potty options available to the paddling public:

A molded-plastic holding tank. This comes with aluminum handles, a hard plastic seat assembly, and easy-to-clean parts.

A stainless-steel holding tank. This comes with an automatic pressure release valve and an opening for freshwater flushing. Some models have stout handles at seat level; combined with a square design, this provides stability for those on the throne.

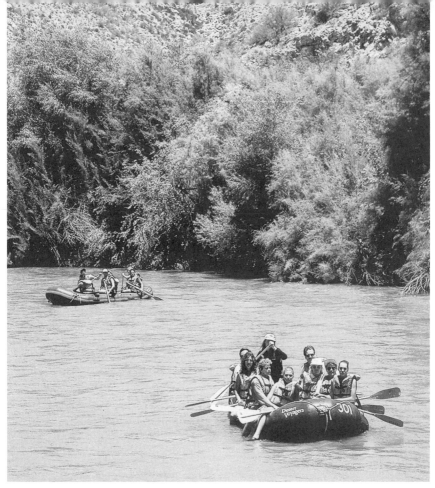

Rafting on the Salt River, Arizona *(Photo by Chris Gould)*

A chemical resistant, laminated fiberglass resin seat tank. This comes with marine-grade fasteners and handles, and a hose fitting that serves as the venting system when in camp.

A stainless-steel box with a standard toilet seat. This fits neatly into any old 20-millimeter "rocket" box. It has a built-in power spray nozzle that blasts the inside when emptying at a dump station, while the quick-release top lid remains sealed, virtually assuring the handler of no unpleasant doo-doo contact.

A lightweight, high-density polyethylene bucket. This has a screw-type transport lid with a safety lock, but no pressure release valve.

A biodegradable pot and lid. Made out of recycled paper, this unique contraption comes with five form-fitting disks that are pressed into place over each day's deposits. To use the device, place the disks inside a five-gallon pickle pail and put the toilet seat on top.

No matter which type you decide on, keep in mind that before you head down the river with the latrine in tow, you should find out from the land manager where you can properly empty your potty at the end of your trip. Also, be strategic about where you place the potty in camp since the trek to the throne gets lots of traffic. Try to put it on a well-established path or a durable gravel bar.

Because of the high number of people traveling and camping along a river corridor, the stench of urine can sometimes be a problem on popular waterways. The solution in some cases, such as in the Grand Canyon, is a land management policy that instructs visitors to pee directly in the water. This is thought to be an environmentally sound practice in any large, high volume, silty western river with a flow of 500 cubic feet per second (cfs) or more. Wastewater can be dumped in the river also.

Outside of the Grand Canyon, check with land managers on their pee policies. Putting any kind of waste in rivers is against the law in some states. On rivers and in places where the flow is slow, walk a good distance away from camp to do your peeing. Wastewater should be strained and sumped.

Reducing Impact

Be sure to lash down everything in your boat. In the event of capsizing, you will save your gear and prevent sending expensive litter downriver.

If you decide to go for an exploratory hike away from camp, stick to established trails—which are certain to exist at well-used sites.

LNT Basics: Canoeing and Rafting

Making Camp
▲ Try to camp in the river's floodplain (unless there is risk of flooding), and check with land managers about designated sites.
▲ Control litter by repackaging foods before the trip and putting down a tarp in the camp cooking area to catch debris.
▲ Avoid having a campfire. If you do, use a fire pan and bring wood with you or pick up driftwood for fuel over the course of the day.

Waste Disposal
▲ On remote, rarely visited waterways, bury your waste in a cat hole 200 feet from shore.
▲ If you are traveling through a narrow, slickrock river corridor or in a popular area, pack out your solid waste. Follow land management policy.
▲ Check with land managers about pee policies. On some silty western rivers, you can urinate in the waterway; otherwise, pee well away from shore and campsites.

Reducing Impact
▲ Secure your load in the boat to avoid littering in the event of capsizing.
▲ Be aware of trampling vegetation, and follow established trails when venturing away from the river corridor.

Chapter 8

Special Environments
LNT GUIDELINES FOR ARCTIC TUNDRA, ALPINE TUNDRA, DESERTS, AND ARCHAEOLOGICAL SITES

hen author and eco-warrior Edward Abbey wrote *Desert Solitaire* in the mid-1960s, it was something of a novelty to celebrate hiking in the harsh environs of the desert. Back then, the deserts and other wilderness areas considered a "no man's land" were backcountry destinations only for the eccentric. While Abbey was wandering alone among the cacti, most hikers stuck to the picture-postcard places—the alpine meadows, lush forests, and backcountry lakes.

Abbey was ahead of his time. As more and more people ventured into the wilderness, the farther afield folks traveled to find solitude and a sense of adventure. Places generally considered inhospitable to humans became sought-after destinations, from the frozen Arctic, to windblown mountaintops, to the arid desert. Now these extreme environments are on the must-visit list for many wilderness travelers, and people are crowding spots that Ed Abbey used to explore all by his lonesome.

Arctic tundra, alpine tundra (above tree line), and deserts have several things in common: the harsh terrain is not conducive to supporting human life, and—compared to all other types of landscapes—the terrain is least able to withstand incursions from human visitors. When hikers travel across tundra or sensitive desert soils, the trampling impact can last several hundred years, compared to years or decades in a forest or meadow environment.

This does not mean that human visitors necessarily should stay away from these sensitive environments. On the contrary, there is no place I would rather be backpacking than in the scenic desert wilderness areas of Arizona and southern Utah. But visiting these places requires an understanding of the fragile environment in which you are traveling and knowledge of LNT skills aimed specifically at minimizing your impact there.

Guidelines follow for hiking and camping in tundra and desert landscapes,

U.S. Fish and Wildlife Service and Bureau of Land Management

Two Agencies with Multiple-Use Missions But Plenty of Wilderness

When most people plan a backcountry trip, they may only consider visiting Forest Service or National Park Service lands. What they may not know, however, is that the U.S. Fish and Wildlife Service and the Bureau of Land Management have plenty of backcountry areas that are excellent recreation destinations—and they typically have far fewer visitors.

Preserves managed by the U.S. Fish and Wildlife Service may be less heavily inundated by human visitors, but the refuges see plenty of traffic from feathered species. Established by Congress in 1956 to run the nation's wildlife refuge system, the Fish and Wildlife Service currently oversees the management of 90 million acres in seventy-five preserves. However, 85 percent (77 million acres) of the refuge system is in Alaska. Refuges in the Lower 48 states are primarily located along the four major North American flyways—Atlantic, Central, Mississippi, and Pacific—and are critical rest stops for migrating birds.

Although these national wildlife refuges were established to protect shrinking habitat for certain species, "secondary uses" allowed on many of the preserves—such as hunting, off-road vehicle recreation, and water skiing—are harmful to wildlife. For example, military bombing exercises regularly conducted on the Cabeza Prieta National Wildlife Refuge in Arizona are the source of major stress for antelope and other wildlife; proposed oil drilling on the Arctic National Wildlife Refuge in Alaska would threaten, among other species, migrating caribou herds.

The Bureau of Land Management (BLM) oversees 272 million acres, which is a larger portion of federal lands (about 45 percent) than the holdings of any other agency. Located almost entirely in the western Lower 48 states and Alaska, the vast BLM holdings comprise what is left of the public domain and can generally be characterized as the "leftover lands"—the land that was too inhospitable to be homesteaded and lacking in lush, loggable forests or any notable "crown jewel"–type features that would make it worthy of becoming a national park. However, for lovers of solitude and wild places, BLM lands offer a wealth of recreation destinations.

Established in 1946 when Congress merged the U.S. Grazing Service and General Land Office, the BLM historically has been involved in the business of managing federal real estate for the benefit of private ranchers and mining companies. It was not until the passage of the Federal Land Policy and Management Act in 1976 that the BLM was formally discharged of the 150-year-old duty of "disposing" of the public domain. The landmark law gave the BLM statutory authority to retain and manage all that was left of the public domain in the best interest of its owners—the public. The law also instructed the BLM to inventory its holdings for lands that should be added to the National Wilderness Preservation System, a charge from which the agency was excluded when the Wilderness Act was passed in 1964.

Over the past two decades, recreation has been a growing component of the BLM's multiple-use mandate. These undeveloped lands, especially in the Southwest, are increasingly popular destinations for backpacking, mountain biking, and camping, among other activities. Currently, BLM holdings encompass some 470 developed recreation sites and more than 2000 miles of trails. The agency is the steward of the 1.7-million-acre Grand Staircase–Escalante National Monument located in southern Utah, the 1.2-million-acre Grand Canyon–Parashant National Monument in Arizona, and a host of other "wilderness"-quality national monuments established by former President Bill Clinton.

along with some pointers for minimizing impact around archaeological sites. Primarily found in southwestern deserts, these ancient ruins are irreplaceable and highly susceptible to decay. Consequently, the presence of these cultural treasures makes an already fragile environment that much more vulnerable to human influence.

Arctic Tundra

Treeless, level, or rolling ground in polar regions is known as arctic tundra. This terrain occupies 10 percent of the earth's surface area, with a large part of that amount found in Alaska and Canada. Arctic tundra is a polar desert of sorts; the sparse vegetation has a growing season only two to four months long and precipitation is usually less than 15 inches per year.

Existing at high latitudes, an arctic tundra ecosystem is subjected to long periods of sunlight in summer and darkness in winter, and extreme temperature fluctuations—sometimes going from 40 degrees Fahrenheit in summer to minus 25 degrees in winter. Plant life that can live in this harsh climate includes hearty species such as lichens, mosses, small herbs, and low shrubs. Animals common to arctic tundra are the polar bear, arctic fox, arctic wolf, arctic weasel, and caribou. As anyone who has visited the Arctic National Wildlife Refuge in summer knows, mosquitoes and blackflies seem more plentiful in an arctic tundra environment than anywhere else on the planet.

Although the arctic tundra landscape generally stays frozen year-round, the top layer of soil thaws in the summer months, causing water to permeate down to

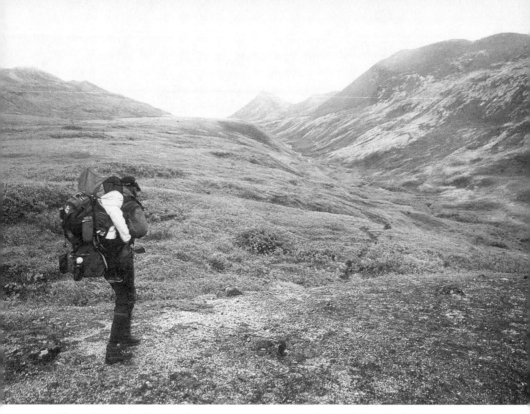

The author carries her sleeping son across arctic tundra in Denali State Park, Alaska.
(Photo by Mike Frick)

an ice and soil barrier called permafrost. Because the water has nowhere to go, it stays pooled just above the permafrost barrier, causing the top, thawed layer of soil to be quite mushy. It is during this thaw period that most of the biological activity that sustains the tundra ecosystem takes place: animals burrow into the soil, plant roots extend down, and organic matter decomposes into food or microorganisms. The web of life in an arctic tundra environment is very delicate, and human visitors can easily upset any of these processes, thereby causing a domino effect that will degrade the ecosystem.

Traveling on Arctic Tundra

Aside from the fact that slogging through wet tundra makes for very difficult hiking, the potential for eroding this fragile landscape is extreme. Areas blanketed with sensitive vegetation such as lichen beds or woody, stemmed ground covers are the most at risk. Researchers studying visitor impacts in Alaska's central Brooks Range found, for example, that once hikers trampled a lichen colony, soil beds that took hundreds of years to develop were lost to erosion.

The unique way in which arctic tundra erodes from trampling is called *thermokarsting*. When protective ground cover plants are destroyed, it exposes the soil to more sunlight and causes too many ice crystals in the permafrost layer to melt. Because ice has a higher volume than water, the unnatural thawing causes the top soil layer to sink, and makes it nearly impossible for vegetation to ever reestablish itself. Once thermokarsting occurs, it is likely a permanent change to the landscape.

In her book *Midnight Wilderness*, Debbie Miller talks about encountering thermokarsting in the early 1990s while walking across the tundra in Alaska's Arctic National Wildlife Refuge. The scars from a truck that drove through the area in the 1950s were clearly visible and its tracks had eroded into the soil about 6 inches.

Practicing the LNT principle of "camp and travel on durable surfaces" is critical when visiting an arctic tundra environment, but a durable surface is not always easy to find. Unfortunately, the summer months that are most hospitable to humans are also the time when the land is at its mushiest state and most susceptible to trampling.

Whenever possible, hike on established trails. In the absence of established pathways, seek out boulder-strewn streambeds as the next best durable surface for your route. If, after considering all the options, you find it necessary to travel across the tundra, try to walk on ground that is dry and covered with grasses or sedges rather than low shrubs or lichen beds. As in other places, when traveling cross-country on arctic tundra, spread out rather than walking single file and try to stick to durable surfaces like snow or rock.

Making Camp

The terrain that is most suitable for hiking in an arctic tundra environment is also the best choice for camp. If you have the option of camping at an established site, do so. However, the chances of finding established campsites in most arctic wilderness areas are not great, and the next best option is to camp in the gravel bed of a stream drainage—as long as you take precautions against flash floods and are at least 200 feet from the water.

If flooding is a possibility or there is no stream where you are traveling, seek out a patch of mineral soil (sand or gravel) to camp on for the night. On many tundra landscapes that are slightly hilly, soil slippage is a common occurrence, and exposed mineral soil makes for a durable and comfortable campsite.

Because of the lack of downed wood and the fragile soils on most arctic tundra landscapes, fires are inappropriate. Bring a camp stove for cooking and plenty of adequate clothing and gear for warmth.

Waste Disposal

Arctic wilderness is one of the few places on the planet where smearing feces can be the best poop placement option. Because tundra soils are so fragile and often frozen, digging a cat hole can be problematic.

Surface disposal should be used only if visitation to the region is low, you are visiting the tundra environment during summer when there is plenty of sunlight to speed decomposition—and you can't dig a decent cat hole. Choose a spot for smearing that is 200 feet from marsh or bog areas so the water is not contaminated.

When visiting a popular area in the Arctic, dispose of waste in a cat hole whenever possible. If the ground is frozen, however, packing it out may prove to be the most environmentally responsible option.

Alpine Tundra

While arctic tundra is found at high latitudes, alpine tundra environments exist at high altitudes—in mountain ranges above tree line. You will encounter alpine tundra on many mountaintops in the Lower 48, including the White Mountains, the Adirondacks, the Rockies, the Sierras, and the Cascades. Like arctic tundra, this alpine landscape is treeless and most of the ecosystem-sustaining processes take place during a brief summer thaw period. The primary differences between alpine and arctic landscapes are that alpine soils are not perennially frozen and the precipitation is greater.

Because of harsh conditions, including wind gusts that can be hurricane force and a regular battering of lightning strikes, life above tree line is impossible for most species. There are, however, some hearty flora and fauna that manage to survive, and even thrive.

The most characteristic vegetation marking the boundaries of alpine tundra is called *krummholz*—twisted, dwarflike trees that are often thousands of years old. In addition to the diminutive and ancient trees, alpine tundra often harbors shrubs, lichens, and various types of wildflowers.

Alpine animals are only partially adapted to their harsh tundra environment and either migrate down-mountain or hibernate during winter. Species in alpine environs include mountain goats, bobcats, marmots, and voles. Because of the struggle these plants and animals must endure just to survive, any kind of disturbance from human visitors can have severe consequences.

Traveling Above Tree Line

From the White Mountains to the Colorado Rockies to the Sierra Nevada, it is the nature of alpine trails to be comprised of an endless chain of switchbacks to the summit. It is human nature to try to take a quicker route by shortcutting up the switchbacks and pioneering "volunteer" trails. On popular summit trails, these renegade paths can literally destroy the delicate alpine tundra environment. Researchers in Rocky Mountain National Park, for example, estimate that alpine tundra disturbed by informal trails could take several hundred to a thousand years to recover—even if the paths are never used again.

Hikers should stay on the trail no matter where they are, but it is imperative

Above tree line in New Hampshire *(Photo by Robert Kozlow)*

when traveling through alpine tundra. The fragile vegetation and microclimates beneath rocks simply cannot withstand human disturbance. Wear gaiters—and crampons, if necessary—so you can walk through mud, snow, and ice on the trail rather than around it. Staying on the trail is a land management regulation in various popular alpine destinations, including the White Mountains in New Hampshire and Arizona's San Francisco Peaks.

Making Camp

In general, places above tree line do not make ideal campsites, because of the wind and exposure to lightning, and because it is nearly impossible to spend the night on fragile alpine tundra without negatively impacting the environment.

If you find it necessary to pitch your tent above tree line, however, try to do it at an established site. In popular mountain ranges it is common to find campsites near the top with boulders moved around and a telltale fire ring. When an established site is not available, choose a resistant surface such as snow, rock, or mineral soil. Avoid disturbing vegetation and do not move rocks around—these are important microhabitats in an alpine tundra environment.

Also, because of the typically strong gusts of wind on mountaintops, pay close attention to keeping track of your trash and gear. A food wrapper or even a free-standing tent can quickly become airborne and sail off the mountain. As in the arctic tundra environment, campfires are a bad idea above tree line due to the lack of fuel and the sensitive soils.

Waste Disposal

Surface disposal—or smearing—in theory can work in an alpine tundra setting for all the same reasons that it works in the arctic, but in reality it is not a good choice on mountaintops. There are too many people climbing around on popular peaks, and nobody wants to encounter someone else's smear. Consequently, on most popular mountains, such as Mount Shasta and El Capitan in California, land managers require hikers and climbers to pack out their poop. Even if it is not required, packing it out is likely the best option in alpine tundra. An alternative is hiking down to tree line or into a side canyon and finding suitable mineral or organic soil for digging a cat hole.

Deserts

From the lush, botanical garden–type environment in Arizona's Organ Pipe Cactus National Monument, to the endless plain of dry mudflats in California's Death Valley, desert terrain varies dramatically in the United States. But the one thing the 500,000 square miles of desert in North America share is a scarcity of water. Just as the limited warmth makes tundra environments so fragile, limited water in the desert makes life precarious for plants and animals in these arid lands. As in tundra environments, the balance of life in desert ecosystems is far too delicate to withstand human impacts when the struggle to survive is already tough enough.

Deserts in North America generally fall into five regions—all located west of the Mississippi. These various desert environments have their own unique vegetation, climate, and terrain. When planning a desert backcountry trip, it is helpful to have an understanding of the environmental characteristics of the area in which you will be traveling so you can be prepared to practice LNT principles. Here is a summary of the desert regions you might visit:

Great Basin. The coldest, highest, largest, and northernmost of our continent's deserts, the Great Basin encompasses most of Nevada and Utah, and extends into southeastern Oregon, southern Idaho, southwestern Wyoming, the northwestern corner of Colorado, and a small portion of northern Arizona. Temperatures in the Great Basin are lower than in other deserts, and periods of freezing temperatures are not uncommon in winter. Great Basin vegetation is characterized by gray-green sagebrush and shadscale; these low-lying shrubs cover hundreds of square miles in continuous sweeps.

Mohave Desert. Situated primarily in southeastern California, the Mohave Desert is something of a transition zone between the Great Basin to the north and the Sonoran Desert to the south. Creosote bush is the predominant vegetation in this sparse desert, but the distinctive Joshua tree is, perhaps, what gives the region the most notoriety. Joshua Tree National Park is a popular rock-climbing destination in the Mohave.

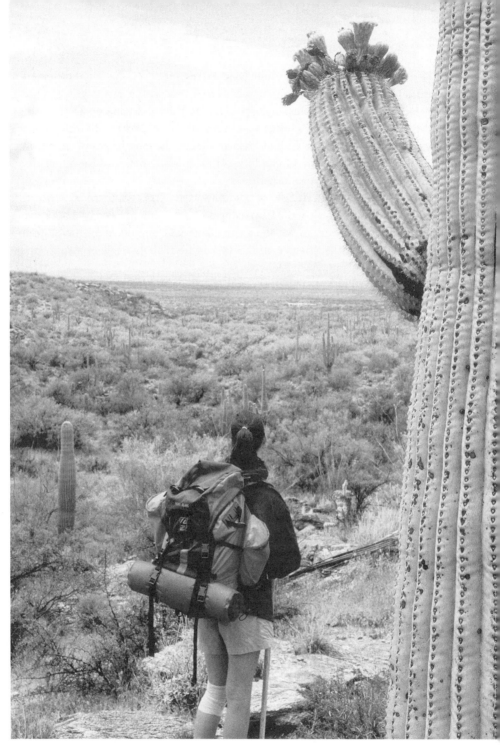

Sonoran desert, Arizona *(Photo by Mike Frick)*

Sonoran Desert. When Hollywood makes a western, the Sonoran Desert is usually the backdrop. The Sonoran Desert is rich with a variety of vegetation, including the saguaro cactus, organ pipe cactus, palo verde, and many other spiny plants. The region spans southern and central Arizona, Baja California, and the northwestern coast of the Gulf of Mexico. Among the most beautiful destinations in the Sonoran Desert are Organ Pipe National Monument and the Superstition Mountain Wilderness Area in Arizona.

Chihuahuan Desert. Spanning southwestern Texas, southern New Mexico, and north-central Mexico, the Chihuahuan Desert is not as dry as the other types of desert environments. Yucca and agave plants are common, as are mesquite and prickly pear cactus. Big Bend National Park in Texas offers excellent hiking opportunities in the Chihuahuan Desert.

Colorado Plateau. This arid region encompassing northern Arizona, southern Utah, northwestern New Mexico, and southwestern Colorado is actually a combination of Great Basin and Mohave Desert environments, but it has a character all its own. In fact, this high desert landscape, with its colorful sandstone arches, dramatic canyons, and scenic riparian corridors, probably receives more backcountry visitors than all other desert areas combined. Popular destinations in this region include Arizona's Grand Canyon National Park, Utah's Zion and Canyonlands National Parks, and numerous national monuments established to preserve ancient Native American cultural sites.

Desert Travel

For people who are unfamiliar with desert environments, the clumpy black soil called cryptobiotic crust looks insignificant. But, in fact, these irregularly raised pedestals in the sand are self-sustaining biological communities that are essential to the ecology of arid lands. Cryptobiotic crusts (also called *cryptogam* or *cryptogamic soil*) prevent erosion, enrich the soil, and allow new plants to take root. A mature cryptobiotic garden can take hundreds of years to develop, and human trampling can destroy it in just a few seconds. These delicate crusts are most prevalent on the Colorado Plateau, but are also common in the Sonoran Desert and Great Basin regions.

The number one priority when traveling in the desert is to avoid stepping on cryptobiotic soil. It is not hard to do if you are looking out for this distinctive ground cover. The best option, from an LNT perspective, is to faithfully hike on established trails. If you find yourself in a region without trails, slickrock and gravel or sand washes are the most durable and suitable surfaces.

Also, try to minimize unnecessary hiking by being prepared. Check with land managers ahead of time about water availability in the region you are visiting, and pack in plenty of water. If you have enough water and/or you know where to find an adequate water source, you can avoid a lot of senseless and destructive roaming

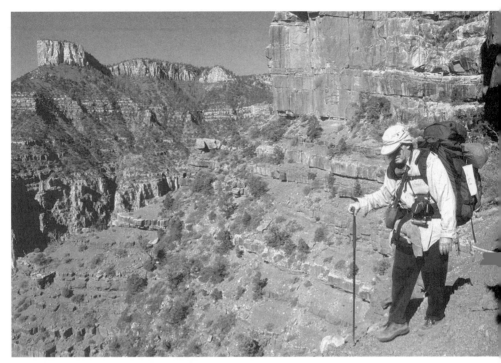
Desert rat hiking the Grand Canyon *(Photo by Elias Butler)*

around looking for the elusive H_2O. Most desert travelers should plan on carrying at least one gallon of water per person per day on a desert trek.

Make sure you are familiar with the trail and route, so you do not get lost and find yourself standing in the middle of a giant patch of cryptobiotic crust.

Making Camp

The same criteria used for desert travel also apply to finding a minimum-impact campsite. Whenever possible, camp at an established site. If that is not an option, find a durable spot on mineral soil (gravel or sand) or rock. A freestanding tent can come in handy on desert treks because many of the comfortable and durable campsites are located on smooth expanses of slickrock.

Campfires are generally inappropriate in desert environments due to the lack of downed wood. Even if you do find a scattering of juniper or cedar branches lying around, they are likely the irreplaceable homes of a variety of desert critters. Bring warm clothing and a camp stove, however, to keep yourself warm on chilly desert nights when the temperature drops dramatically from the daytime high.

According to Pam Foti, a professor in the Parks and Recreation Management Program at Northern Arizona University, campfires have no place in the desert. After monitoring recreation impacts on public lands in Arizona and southern

Travel on Durable Surfaces

▲ **Arctic tundra:** Whenever possible, hike on established trails. In the absence of established pathways, seek out boulder-strewn streambeds. If you find it necessary to travel across the tundra, try to walk on ground that is dry and covered with grasses or sedges rather than low shrubs or lichen beds.

▲ **Alpine tundra:** Stay on established trails and avoid "volunteer" paths. Wear gaiters—and crampons, if necessary—so you can walk through mud, snow, and ice on the trail rather than around it.

▲ **Desert:** Avoid stepping on cryptobiotic soil—black, clumpy ground cover that is self-sustaining biological communities. Hike on established trails. If you find yourself in a region without established trails, slickrock and gravel or sand washes are the most durable surfaces.

Making Camp

▲ **Arctic tundra:** Camp at an established site if you can. The next best option is to camp in the gravel bed of a stream drainage or on exposed mineral soil in the fold of a hill.

▲ **Alpine tundra:** In general, places above tree line don't make ideal campsites. But if you find it necessary to pitch your tent above tree line, try to do it at an established site. When an established site isn't available, choose a resistant surface such as snow, rock, or mineral soil.

▲ **Desert:** Camp at established sites. If you find yourself in a region without established campsites, slickrock, gravel, and sand are the most durable surfaces. (But don't camp in washes because of the danger of flash floods.)

▲ The lack of downed wood, slow plant growth, and fragile soils make fires inappropriate in most tundra and desert environments.

Conserve Water in the Desert

▲ Most desert hikers should carry at least one gallon of water per person per day.

▲ Avoid disrupting wildlife and their access to scarce water sources. Unless you are camped near a perennial stream or river, extract water from area sources only for drinking.

▲ Small water sources are inappropriate for bathing. Even if you do not use soap, these water sources are easily polluted by humans.

Properly Dispose of Human Waste

▲ **Arctic tundra:** Dig a cat hole if possible. If not, smearing feces may be the best poop placement option; surface disposal should be used only if visitation to the region is low and you are visiting the tundra environment during summer when there is plenty of sunlight to speed decomposition. If you are visiting a popular area, dispose of waste in a cat hole or pack it out.

▲ **Alpine tundra:** Even if it is not required, packing out poop is likely the best option. An alternative is to hike down to tree line or into a side canyon and find suitable soil for digging a cat hole.

▲ **Desert:** Cat holes are the preferred option in most desert landscapes. Make sure the hole is at least 200 feet away from water sources or washes and gullies that could fill with water after a rain. Pack it out in narrow canyons.

Utah for a decade, she's tired of seeing the damaged vegetation, rock scars, and dead soil left by campers wanting the aesthetics of a warm glow. "Campfires are the number one impact in the Southwest," Foti says. "There's no way to justify the environmental damage caused by a fire unless it's an emergency."

Desert visitors also must be careful not to disrupt wildlife and their access to the area's precious few water sources. Unless you are camped near a perennial stream or river, extract water from area sources only for drinking. A *tinaja*—a puddle of water in a rock depression—may not look like much to humans, but it is a wildlife oasis and can easily be depleted by one camping party. If you're in an area where there are only tinajas or a few small springs, the most environmentally responsible thing to do is pack in all your H_2O and leave the natural water sources for wildlife. In fact, it's a requirement in some desert parks such as Big Bend and Organ Pipe.

Waste Disposal

Despite the fact that it was something of an (ill-advised) LNT fad about ten years ago, surface disposal of human waste is not recommended in desert environments. Visitation to our nation's arid lands has increased so dramatically over the last decade that few people will find themselves in a location remote enough for smearing.

Cat holes are the preferred option in most desert landscapes. Keep in mind that your deposit will be there for a long time because decomposition is very slow. Make sure the hole is at least 200 feet away from water sources or washes and gullies that could fill with water after a rain. In narrow Southwest canyons where it's often impossible to get 200 feet from a drainage, the best option is to pack it out—a requirement in the Zion Narrows and soon to be required in Paria Canyon.

No matter how sweaty you are, small water sources such as tinajas or springs are inappropriate to use for bathing. Even if you are not using soap, these precious few water sources are easily polluted by human body oils and topical applications like sunscreen. Desert animals rely on these for drinking water, so do not use them for bathing.

Archaeological and Historical Sites

From Civil War battlefields on the East Coast, to ancient Ancestral Puebloan ruins on the Colorado Plateau, to Native American petroglyphs in the Pacific Northwest, our nation's wildlands harbor many historic and prehistoric cultural treasures. Technically, these sites are protected under the Archaeological Resources Protection Act of 1979 and the Antiquities Protection Act of 1906. It is a federal offense to disturb or destroy archaeological and historic sites, and many people have been sent to jail for doing so.

The problem is that many of these sites are in remote backcountry areas, and illegal activity can occur virtually unmonitored. An even bigger problem, however, is that most damage inflicted on our nation's cultural treasures is done so unknowingly by well-meaning wilderness travelers who just want to have a closer look.

The desert environments in the Southwest are especially vulnerable to vandalism of archaeological sites. The dramatic increase in backcountry visitation to public lands on the Colorado Plateau, combined with the concentration of archaeological sites in the region, for example, is making a delicate environment that much more vulnerable to human impacts.

"The ruins and rock art of the Southwest are being loved to death," notes Rick Moore of the nonprofit group Grand Canyon Trust. "It is difficult to convince people that seemingly innocent acts that have no perceptible impact can be severely damaging over time. The cumulative effect of a thousand light touches to a wall makes it fall apart."

Some of the destruction to archaeological sites in the Southwest is blatant vandalism, but most of it is due to what Moore called "innocent acts that destroy." The loss is great because many of the Indian ruins and rock art in the region date back to before Columbus set foot in America, and some date back to before Christ.

If you happen to be hiking and camping in an area with archaeological sites, use the following guidelines to observe the Leave No Trace principle of "Leave what you find" and protect these treasures for future generations:

- As you approach an archaeological site, stop for a moment and think about how you can minimize your impact. Stay off the midden, usually a low mound

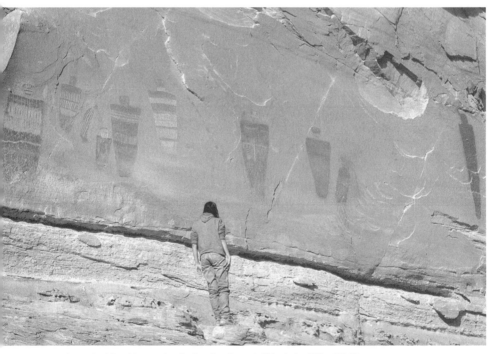

Ancestral Puebloan ruins in the Southwest *(Photo by Mike Frick)*

near the site, which was the original inhabitants' trash pile and holds valuable information for archaeologists.

▲ Stay on established trails around the site and avoid walking along the base of walls built on slopes. Erosion will make them topple.

▲ Walls that are stressed once too often can collapse. Do not use them as handholds to gain access to a site, and do not stand or climb on them.

▲ Try to camp at least 200 feet from archaeological sites.

▲ Do not pick up any artifact. If you do accidentally move something (like a potsherd), put it back exactly where you found it.

▲ Charcoal and soot remains are used to carbon-date sites. Modern charcoal and soot contaminate the ancient record, so do not build campfires near a site.

▲ Do not touch rock art; oils from human skin can cumulatively destroy mineral-based paints.

▲ Children's natural curiosity and enthusiasm for climbing can be aroused by the walls, nooks, and crannies found at most sites. Hold youngsters' hands while visiting, and explain to them the reasons for not exploring too vigorously.

In general, the Leave No Trace principle of "leave what you find" means don't touch. This applies everywhere—whether you are tempted to touch rock art in Canyonlands National Park, pick up a piece of petrified wood in the Painted Desert, or pocket a metal buckle lying on the ground at Gettysburg.

LNT Basics: Minimizing Impacts to Archaeological and Historical Sites

▲ As you approach an archaeological site, stay off the midden, which is usually a low mound near the site. This was the original inhabitants' trash pile and holds valuable information for archaeologists.

▲ Stay on established trails around the site and avoid walking along the base of walls built on slopes. Erosion will make them topple.

▲ Walls that are stressed once too often can collapse. Do not use them as handholds to gain access to a site, and do not stand or climb on them.

▲ Try to camp at least 200 feet away from archaeological sites.

▲ Do not pick up any artifact. If you do accidentally move something, put it back exactly where you found it.

▲ Charcoal and soot remains are used to date sites. The ancient record is contaminated by modern charcoal and soot, so do not build campfires near a site.

▲ Do not touch rock art; oils from human skin can cumulatively destroy mineral-based paints.

▲ Hold youngsters' hands while visiting and explain to them why they should stay off the site.

Chapter 9

Sharing the LNT Message
TEACHING MINIMUM IMPACT TECHNIQUES TO KIDS, FRIENDS, AND STRANGERS

If a rattlesnake bit your hiking partner, would you cut the wound and try to suck the venom out? Have you ever taken salt tablets in an effort to stay hydrated during strenuous activity? Would you give a shivering friend whiskey to help warm him up?

Anyone familiar with wilderness medicine practices knows the answer to each of these questions should be a hearty "no." Modern science has debunked these old-time remedies as the stuff of medical myth, useful only for making people feel worse.

But if you were uneducated in first aid, and you grew up in an environment where people swore by these kinds of folk remedies, how would you know the "cut and suck" method only promotes infection in a snakebite victim? If someone told you that much of what you'd been taught about how to care for ailing people in the backcountry was wrong, you might not respond very favorably.

I view Leave No Trace as a kind of preventive medicine and first aid for the land. Up-to-date knowledge of certain principles and learned skills promotes environmental health. People who know these skills are no better than the people who don't know them; they are just better informed. There is also a certain universal environmental ethic behind LNT, just as there is a humanitarian ethic behind

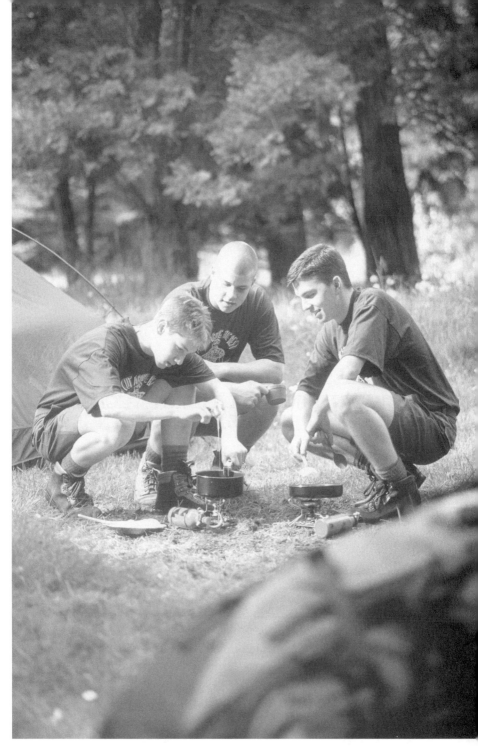

Today Boy Scouts learn Leave No Trace practices. *(Photo courtesy of Boy Scouts of America)*

wilderness medicine. Most people want to help protect the wilderness, not destroy it—just as they would want to assist an injured person they encounter along the trail.

In the majority of instances where human visitation is damaging wildlands, it is not due to maliciousness but rather a lack of knowledge about how to protect the health of these special places. Many people are still unaware that traditional camping and backcountry travel practices used for generations damage the environment. Because many more wildland visitors hit the trail every weekend than there are land managers available to counsel them, it is highly unlikely that these people will change their high-impact ways based on a chance encounter with a ranger.

The future success of Leave No Trace—and of wildland preservation in general—depends on education, and on the ability of backcountry users to educate each other in the new wilderness etiquette. The best place to begin this education, of course, is in the home, with your family. Now that you've read this book, you have become knowledgeable in Leave No Trace skills and, hopefully, have the desire to share that knowledge with others. What follows are some suggestions on how to educate your children, your friends, and even strangers on the trail about minimum-impact techniques.

Teaching LNT Practices to Kids

Not so long ago, the Boy Scout Handbook offered detailed information on how to disturb and destroy the wilderness landscape. That was not the authors' intention, of course, but standard camping practices in the 1960s and before were inevitably high-impact—including those of the Boy Scouts.

Children were taught that good campers dug a trench around their tent, cut tree boughs for a bed, built a roaring campfire, and buried their trash when they vacated the site. Those young campers grew up to be adult campers, and the Leave No Trace program has been reaching out to these people in an effort to teach them camping practices that are more environmentally responsible.

In addition to helping longtime wilderness users learn new camping tricks, a major component of the Leave No Trace program is teaching children proper minimum-impact skills from the start. Today, the Boy Scout Handbook offers detailed information on how to practice the principles of Leave No Trace, and all those circa-1960s high-impact campcraft skills are considered ancient history. The new Boy Scout Handbook of advanced outdoor skills devotes one of its five sections entirely to Leave No Trace techniques. Over the last decade, the Leave No Trace ethic became an important part of the Boy Scout philosophy, and efforts are underway across the country to teach everyone from troop leaders to young Cub Scouts the latest in environmental responsibility and minimum-impact techniques.

Along with the Boy Scouts, many other outdoor organizations and land management offices have committed to teaching the new wilderness etiquette to children. Conservation-minded adults recognize that the future prospects for protecting wildlands through Leave No Trace ethics are only as good as the minimum-impact skills of our future wilderness users—today's children.

LNT practices are taught to children through three primary venues: schools, youth-oriented outdoor programs, and role models, including parents, siblings, relatives, and family friends. If you work with children in a group setting and want to teach them LNT principles, or if you would just like to inspire your own child with a minimum-impact ethic, keep in mind the following hints:

Kids like to do things. A child's world is full of discovery, and learning about nature and LNT practices should be an active process. Contests and games are effective teaching methods. Also, introduce an element of excitement into the activity whenever possible. For example, go for a walk at night and listen for owls. See who can wash dishes with the least amount of water. March through the mud on a trail, rather than around it.

Tell stories, don't preach. There is no better way to lose the attention of children than to lecture them. If you are not teaching them through an activity, then make it into a story. For example, if you want a child to understand why food scraps should not be thrown on the ground, tell a tale about a mother fox and her kits who learned to live off garbage instead of hunting for their dinner. When the garbage was gone, the fox family went hungry because they did not know how to hunt.

Look for "teachable moments." If you are in the backcountry, you will likely encounter many situations along the way that illustrate Leave No Trace principles. Pointing out trail erosion, for example, and showing the lack of vegetation around the disturbed area is a much more effective way to teach the "camp and travel on durable surfaces" principle than just explaining it hypothetically.

Have fun. According to John Gookin, NOLS curriculum manager, it is important to not take things too seriously. "If I had cautionary advice," he said in an LNT newsletter article, "it would be to carefully balance and integrate the learning with fun and, especially, raw adventure. Kids do not want to waste their time learning to pass some written test; they want to learn cool stuff that their friends will think is neat."

Help kids feel connected to nature. Because most children grow up in a relatively urban environment, the undeveloped backcountry can seem very foreign. In order for a child to understand why nature should be protected, he or she needs to feel connected to it. When hiking, point out how a tree has skin just like humans do. When drinking tap water at home, explain that it comes from rivers and lakes in places you may have visited, and keeping those places clean helps keep our drinking water clean. Peek in a fallen log and show your child that insects need a roof over their heads, just like people do.

The LNT program offers a variety of guidance materials for teaching children minimum-impact skills and ethics. Below is a look at some successful LNT education initiatives in use around the country, and additional suggestions on effective ways to teach future wilderness users how to preserve the land.

Schools: Bringing Conservation to the Classroom

He is a gruesome sight—a blaring boom box perched on his shoulder, a cigarette hanging from his mouth, as he vandalizes trail signs and torments wildlife. The "Impact Monster" is a character used in skits to show schoolchildren what is meant, exactly, by bad behavior from an LNT standpoint.

Many Forest Service districts across the United States perform "Impact Monster" skits in local elementary schools to teach young children the basics of Leave No Trace. Skits vary from district to district, but the memorable character is always "noisy, gross, and sloppy." For example, in the skit as performed by the Tonto National Forest's Mesa Ranger District in Mesa, Arizona, the "Impact Monster" throws cigarette butts on the ground, carves graffiti into trail signs, and wraps toilet paper around a saguaro cactus.

According to Tonto National Forest staff member James Munoz, who teaches the LNT message at Mesa schools, the "Impact Monster" skit is most effective with fourth-graders. Willing rangers from the national forest also regularly appear at Mesa area schools to perform a "Woodsy Owl" skit for second-graders and a "Web of Life" ecology program for third-graders, and to promote a Junior Ranger program for older kids.

Like Forest Service youth outreach efforts around the country, the programs developed by Tonto National Forest staff aim to teach children about wilderness preservation and minimum-impact skills before they ever hit the trail. "We concentrate on our future users," says Tonto National Forest administrator Greg Hansen, who helped develop the LNT program in the Mesa district twenty years ago. "Our strategy is to make the educational effort progressive, so the kids keep learning new things every year."

Hansen adds that, to teach children about Leave No Trace, the kids have to be able to relate to the message or it will not hit home. For example, instead of saying it is bad to use soap when washing in a spring because it hurts plant and animal life, his team illustrates the principle graphically. "We take a glass of water and pour dish soap in it," explained Hansen. "Then we hold out the glass and ask the kids if they would drink from it."

In addition to the skits and programs offered to schools by the Forest Service and other land management agencies, the LNT program is also working its way into school curricula. A popular tool used by teachers to illustrate LNT principles and environmental conservation is the "Wilderness Box." Inside this large plastic container are various tools of the LNT trade: a trowel, a fire pan, posters containing LNT principles, animal bones, etc. The teachers are given a syllabus and encouraged to incorporate the curriculum into lesson plans for various subjects instead of trying to deliver the entire LNT message in one "environmental education" class. Overall, those involved in teaching Leave No Trace to schoolchildren say the efforts are most effective when the program is interactive and hands-on.

To get information and materials on the "Impact Monster" skit, the "Wilderness Box," or other educational programs for schools, contact the Leave No Trace Center for Outdoor Ethics (see the appendix).

Outdoor Organizations: The Scoop on the Troops

Leave No Trace principles are incorporated into Boy Scout education programs on many different levels. Every year thousands of youth learn about LNT through the minimum-impact skills camp at Philmont Scout Ranch in New Mexico. Some 35,000 scouts were educated in Leave No Trace at the 2001 National Scout Jamboree held near Fredericksburg, Virginia. In addition, 22,000 scouts have earned the Leave No Trace Award introduced in 1998, and becoming an Eagle Scout now requires demonstration of good LNT techniques.

Troop leaders are trained by LNT Master Educators during an annual workshop at the Philmont Training Center in New Mexico. To further assist troop leaders, Boy Scouts of America published a 120-page book titled *Teaching Leave No Trace* that offers a series of fun activities adults can use to instill LNT principles in youth. Scout leaders—or anyone who wants to teach Leave No Trace to children—can download the entire book free of charge from the organization's website, *www.scouting.org/boyscouts/resources/21-117.*

"As a substantial user of public lands, Boy Scouts of America believes it is imperative that our leaders and youth be trained in Leave No Trace," says Dave Bates, BSA director of camping and conservation. "Instilling values in young people and preparing them to make ethical choices is the mission of Boy Scouts. This dovetails nicely with the Leave No Trace mission of promoting responsible outdoor recreation."

Scouting Ahead is another impressive effort to spread the LNT gospel to young wilderness users. The regional program is a cooperative effort formed ten years ago in the Pacific Northwest by Boy Scouts of America, Girl Scouts of the Puget Sound Area, the Washington Wilderness Coalition, The Mountaineers, and the U.S. Forest Service. Since its inception, more than four hundred troop leaders and eight thousand scouts have participated in the program.

Scouting Ahead has three primary program components:

The Scouting Ahead workshop. Held annually, the workshop trains troop leaders in minimum-impact skills and LNT ethics. The leaders are given a detailed Scouting Ahead manual and coached on how to teach the material to children.

Troop training. Once a leader has completed the workshop and "accepts the LNT challenge," he or she is charged with troop training. The Scouting Ahead manual provides techniques and activities for teaching Leave No Trace principles. Teaching methods include hypothetical problem solving—such as determining from a set of choices the most durable surface on which to camp—and hands-on exercises in, for example, cooking on a small camp stove and learning how to dehydrate foods.

Leave No Trace certification. This annual event is the highlight of the Scouting Ahead program. Both troop leaders and scouts are tested in minimum-impact skills, and those who pass are awarded an LNT merit badge. The daylong certification process involves a written exam and field exercises.

The LNT Song

From Scouting Ahead
(Sung to the tune of "Row, Row, Row Your Boat")

Sack, sack, sack your trash,
Put it in a bag.
Pack it out on your back,
Cause leaving it's a drag.

Sniff, sniff, sniff the flowers,
Leave them where they grow.
Endangered plants you pick today
Your kids may never know.

Camp, camp far away
From the fragile shore,
And when you do you'll save the lake.
It's clean water we're working for.

Cook, cook, cook your food
On a backpack stove.
Save the snags and save the trees
Cause wilderness is gold.

Dig, dig, dig a hole
About 6 inches down;
When nature calls, bury your waste
And leave it underground.

Leave, leave, leave no trace
With your camping gear,
Cause no one, no one in the woods
Wants to see you've been here.

Think, plan, and be aware
In nature's fragile place.
In wilderness we're visitors;
Protect this unspoiled space.

A group of Scouts at Philmont, where they are trained in Leave No Trace
(Photo by Annette McGivney)

According to Adrienne Hall of the Mount Baker-Snoqualmie National Forest, which hosts the LNT certification, the field exercises are rigorous and by the end of the day, most kids are "pretty burned out." The scouts are tested in numerous field demonstrations: they must select the "ten essentials" to put in their backpack, cook a meal and properly dispose of food wastes, choose the proper campsite, take a break along the trail the LNT way, and hike through snow without eroding the trail. "Hands-on activities are by far the most popular way for the scouts to learn about Leave No Trace," Hall says.

A Family Affair: Teaching Your Child LNT Values

The bottom line for teaching children Leave No Trace skills and ethics is that it should start in the home. The minimum-impact approach to wilderness travel is, in a larger sense, an approach to living and therefore something that is most logically handed down to a child from his or her parents.

If you want to instill children with a working knowledge of the new wilderness etiquette, keep in mind that kids (especially young ones) like action. When going on backcountry outings, incorporate activities that help teach LNT principles and spice up the experience. Here are some suggestions:

- ▲ When camping, sit by the light of your flashlight covered with a red bandana and try to identify constellations. Accustom children to spending nights in the backcountry without the glow of a campfire.

- ▲ When hiking, equip each family member with a small plastic bag and have a contest to see who can pick up the most trash. Point out all the "micro-trash" along the trail, such as cigarette butts, food bar wrappers, and even fuzz balls. Make sure children understand, however, not to pick up toilet paper. You can tell them how "icky" and inconsiderate it is for someone to leave something so full of germs in such a beautiful place.

- ▲ When hiking, have a contest to see who can spot the most birds and animals along the way. This helps children understand how many creatures live in the backcountry and depend on a clean environment. Using a field guide, see who can identify the most wildflowers—but don't pick them.

- ▲ When backpacking, let kids choose the campsite, relying on their knowledge of LNT criteria. Write down on an index card what an established site looks like (see Chapter 2, "All About Camping"). After you have set up camp, go on an outing to see if you can find a campsite in which impact is just beginning, then congratulate the kids for making a better choice.

- ▲ Involve children in food planning and preparation. Take them with you to the grocery store to buy ingredients for one-pot meals that will lighten the load in the backpack, require less water, and create less cleanup. Pasta, beans, and couscous are good choices. Make cooking and cleanup a family affair.

- ▲ When in camp, play a game in which your children close their eyes and try to guess what something is by smelling it—soap, a tea bag, gorp. Then explain that animals are strongly guided by their sense of smell, and these odors will draw them into camp if the items are left out.

- ▲ Call your local Forest Service office and see if you and your children can go on a patrol or hike with a wilderness ranger. This is an excellent way for children to visit the front line in the war against human impacts on public lands. Both you and your child will likely be interested in learning what kinds of environmental issues a ranger deals with.

- ▲ Involve children in a local trail cleanup. Hiking clubs and Forest Service ranger districts frequently hold volunteer trail maintenance activities. Make sure the trail work is simple (like picking up trash) and suitable for a child. To find out about trail projects in your area, call local land management offices or inquire at an outdoor retailer about local hiking clubs (see the appendix for some ideas).

- ▲ In the end, of course, there is no more effective method of teaching kids about

Sharing wilderness with a child *(Photo by Robert Kozlow)*

what is important than through your own example. Chances are that if you live by an LNT ethic and strive to minimize impacts wherever you go, so will your children. When grown, they will pass the philosophy on to their children who, hopefully, will have as much wilderness to enjoy as we do today.

LNT Basics: Tips for Teaching Kids LNT Practices

▲ **Kids like to do things.** Learning about nature and LNT practices should be an active process. Contests and games are effective teaching methods, as is anything that incorporates an element of excitement.

▲ **Tell stories, don't preach.** If what you are teaching is not through an activity, then make it into a story.

▲ **Look for "teachable moments."** In the backcountry, you will likely encounter many situations that illustrate Leave No Trace principles. Point out a real-life example of an LNT technique.

▲ **Have fun.** Carefully balance and integrate learning with fun and, especially, raw adventure.

▲ **Help kids feel connected to nature.** When visiting the backcountry, point out common characteristics between the child and the undeveloped surroundings.

Teaching LNT Practices To Grown-Ups

Suggestions on how to educate your friends, as well as strangers you may meet on the trail, in minimum-impact techniques follow.

Teach, don't preach. Think of Leave No Trace as a set of skills that are learned, much as modern first-aid practices are learned. There is no moral high ground that must be taken in order to impart knowledge about basic things such as appropriate backcountry waste disposal or preventing trail erosion. People—especially strangers—are instantly turned off by ethical arguments; just stick with the tangible facts.

Show them "a better way." Never condescend by telling people they are doing something "wrong." Remember, if they are in the backcountry, they are likely there because they enjoy the place as much as you do and do not want to damage it. In communicating the Leave No Trace message, land managers discovered early on that the most effective approach for instructing people was to offer to show them "a better way." In other words, if a party has horses tied to trees, it is not "the wrong way," but you can show them "a better way" to restrain the animals that will not damage vegetation.

Emphasize the "authority of the resource." The Arthur Carhart National Training Center in Montana trains wilderness rangers to influence visitor behavior through the "authority of the resource" instead of the perceived authority that comes with the badge and/or gun they wear. In other words, encourage people to change their behavior based on their desire to help the environment rather than the need to obey an authority figure. "Wilderness areas are among the few places on earth where we have agreed to allow nature, for the most part, to operate on its own terms," says the ranger training manual. "Desirable behavior is more likely to occur if people understand how their actions affect the way nature operates."

As a fellow hiker, rather than a law enforcer, emphasizing the "authority of the resource" is even more important because it is unlikely that people are going to change their behavior just because you say they should. When utilizing the "authority of the resource" technique, focus on environmental impacts over rules and regulations. For example, if you encounter a party with a campfire in an area where fires are banned, explain to them how fires damage soils and strip the land of fallen wood, an essential ingredient to a healthy ecosystem. Then, after the fact, you can throw in that campfires also happen to be against the rules and they could be fined if caught.

What to Do When . . .

Saying we should all become LNT evangelists and spread the minimum-impact gospel is one thing, but actually doing it is another. If you encounter a well-armed hunting party in the woods sitting around a big fire drinking beer, is it a good idea to share with them why campfires are harmful to the environment? Sometimes the situation will not be right for sharing the minimum-impact message. Knowing when and how to approach strangers about Leave No Trace principles can be difficult—and sometimes approaching friends is even tougher. Of course, you will have to rely on your own good judgment in deciding when the time is right to teach LNT practices. Personal safety should never be compromised. However, here are a few hypothetical scenarios to guide you in your evangelical endeavors.

Campfires

Situation: You are on a canoe trip with a group of friends. In camp, they decide to build a warm blaze in the fire ring, so they begin scavenging the area for wood.

Recommended action: The best solution would be to talk to the group about the desire for a campfire before the trip, and plan for it. You can explain to them why it is best, from an environmental standpoint, to rely on a camp stove and not to have a campfire at all. But if advance discussion isn't possible, or if the group couldn't be convinced they should go cold turkey on the campfire idea, then you can suggest techniques for building a fire that will not damage the soil at the campsite or deplete the area of ecologically important fallen logs. Lacking a fire pan, demonstrate how to build a mound fire (see Chapter 2) using small twigs rather than big logs to fuel a cozy blaze.

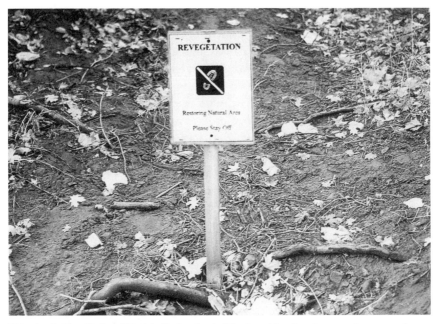

This sign in Zion National Park indicates the trail is closed to allow the area to recover from hiker trampling. *(Photo by Annette McGivney)*

Shortcuts

Situation: You are hiking up a steep trail toward a mountain peak when a group of adolescents on a field trip appears from below after shortcutting up the switchback. They are in a race to the summit and took a shortcut pioneered by other impatient hikers hurrying to reach the top, disregarding the established trail.

Recommended action: Stop the children and ask them to look at the eroded "volunteer" that they just hiked up. Point out that there is no vegetation on or around the rogue path compared to other areas away from the trail. Tell them that the alpine environment is fragile and when they hike off the main trail, they destroy nutrients that plants and animals need in order to live. Also, try to find the group's leader and explain to that person what you have also explained to the children.

Archaeological Sites

Situation: You are backpacking in a remote section of a national park in southern Utah and you encounter a truck backed up to an alcove where there are Native American ruins. There are several people in the alcove and they appear to be digging.

Recommended action: You have likely stumbled upon "pot hunters" who make their living by stealing valuable artifacts from federally owned archaeological sites. They are knowingly breaking the law (violating the Archaeological Resources Protection Act and driving a motorized vehicle into a wilderness area) and may be armed. Do not jeopardize your safety by imparting the "leave what you find" LNT principle to these scoundrels. As inconspicuously as possible, take note of the license plate number and a general description of the people (how many, clothing, etc.), and hike back to the land management office or find a ranger as soon as possible. Tell what you saw and let those in charge of enforcing the law deal with the looters. In vandalism cases, you are more likely to run across people who just don't know any better and are ripe for LNT education. But do not naively assume that everyone acts out of ignorance.

Mountain Bikers

Situation: You are horseback riding in a federal wilderness area and encounter a pair of mountain bikers speeding down the trail.

Recommended action: There is cause for concern here, because the mountain bikers are not only breaking the law by being in a wilderness area, but they could have spooked your horse and caused an accident. Anger, however, gets you nowhere in educating wayward bikers about minimizing their impact.

Be optimistic and assume that the mountain bikers do not know that bikes are disallowed in wilderness areas and possibly do no realize they are in a wilderness area. Call out to the bikers and ask them to stop so you can speak to them. Explain that you are in an area set aside for preservation under the Wilderness Act

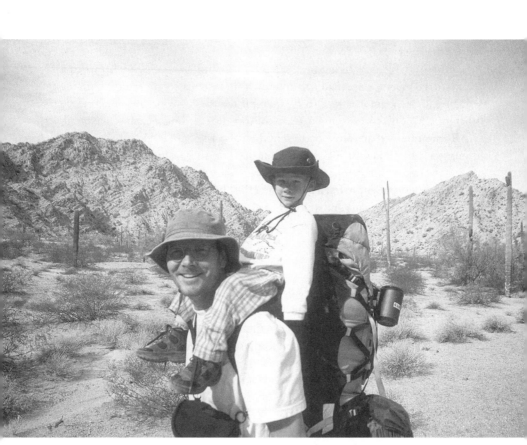

Family backpacking can increase the load for Dad. *(Photo by Annette McGivney)*

(discussed in this book's introduction) and it is off-limits to all mechanized vehicles, including mountain bikes. Add that a speeding bike can startle horses and all of you could have been injured. Hopefully, the mountain bikers will apologize and backtrack slowly out of the wilderness. But if they ignore your advice and keep riding, report the encounter to the land management office when you return to the trailhead.

Adopting a LNT Lifestyle
The new wilderness etiquette outlined in this book is not something you can practice only in the backcountry. Although the Leave No Trace program was designed specifically to address visitor impacts in wildland areas, the ethic behind the seven basic LNT principles is applicable to all aspects of your life—in the office, at home, in the city park, as well as in the backcountry.

Striving to live in a way that minimizes impacts on the environment should involve all types of conservation practices, such as recycling, composting, conserving water, and using public transportation. Even if we never set foot in wilderness areas, a consumptive life in the city ultimately affects those "pristine" places, whether through air pollution, depleting the water table, or an insatiable need for timber to build houses.

Two things are certain in the twenty-first century: the number of people in the United States will continue to grow, and the amount of wilderness in this country will either stay the same or decrease. Consequently, if we are to preserve what wildlands we have left, we can either essentially ban human visitors from the protected areas or we can make LNT practices so pervasive among backcountry users that the prospect of "loving the wilderness to death" is no longer an environmental threat.

The choice seems simple—especially when you think of it in the way conservationist and author Aldo Leopold viewed humankind's relationship to wilderness. "Man always kills the thing he loves, and so we the pioneers have killed our wilderness," wrote Leopold in *A Sand County Almanac*. "Some say we had to. Be that as it may, I am glad I shall never be young without wild country to be young in. Of what avail are forty freedoms without a blank spot on the map?"

LNT Basics: Tips for Teaching Adult LNT Practices

▲ **Teach, don't preach.** Think of Leave No Trace as a set of skills that are learned, much as modern first-aid practices are learned. There is no moral high ground that must be taken in order to impart knowledge about basic things such as appropriate backcountry waste disposal or preventing trail erosion.

▲ **Show them "a better way."** Never condescend by telling a person they are doing something "wrong." In communicating the Leave No Trace message, demonstrate "a better way" rather than condemning environmentally harmful actions.

▲ **Emphasize the "authority of the resource."** Encourage people to change their behavior based on their desire to help the environment rather than the need to obey an authority figure. When utilizing the "authority of the resource" technique, focus on environmental impacts, not rules and regulations.

▲ **Make your home life an example of the LNT ethic.** Strive to minimize impacts on the environment through conservation practices such as recycling, composting, conserving water, and using public transportation. Even if we never set foot in wilderness areas, a consumptive life in the city ultimately affects those "pristine" places.

Appendix
LNT RESOURCES

Leave No Trace Center for Outdoor Ethics
P.O. Box 997
Boulder, CO 80306
(800) 332-4100; (303) 442-8222
www.lnt.org

The Leave No Trace Center is the clearinghouse for all LNT educational materials and public outreach programs, including:

Leave No Trace training courses. Everything from five-day Master Educator courses to half-day workshops are taught by NOLS, AMC, and other LNT partners at locations across the country. Contact the Center for a course schedule or to see about scheduling training for your recreation group.

Educational materials. Some sixteen Skills and Ethics series booklets are available through the Center. The series addresses a variety of different recreation user groups and geographic environments in the United States. The Center also distributes LNT brochures, videos, hangtags, and teaching tools.

Individual membership. Individuals can join Leave No Trace for an annual fee of fifteen dollars or more. Members receive a newsletter and other LNT updates. A children's membership is also available. Begun in 2002, LNT already has more than one thousand individual members through this initiative.

Website. The Leave No Trace website is the central repository for all things LNT. You'll find recreational impact research, wilderness education links, archived newsletters, a directory of LNT Masters, LNT state advocate contacts, and information on all of the above.

◀ Hikers explore the upper reaches of New Hampshire's White Mountains.
(Photo by Robert Kozlow)

Other LNT contacts

The Access Fund (LNT information for climbers)
P.O. Box 17010
Boulder, CO 80308
(303) 545-6772
www.accessfund.org

American Hiking Society
P.O. Box 20160
Washington, DC 20041
(703) 385-3252

Appalachian Mountain Club
Dana Houdek, LNT Program Coordinator
(603) 466-2721, ext. 209
email: *dhoudek@amcinfo.org*
www.amcinfo.org

Backcountry Horsemen of America
P.O. Box 1192
Columbia Falls, MT 59912

Boy Scouts of America
1325 West Walnut Hill Lane
Irving, TX 75015-2079
(972) 580-2000
www.scouting.org

Bureau of Land Management, Utah State Office
Stew Jacobsen, LNT Coordinator
324 South State Street
Salt Lake City, UT 84111
(801) 539-4235
www.blm.gov

The Grand Canyon Trust
Route 4, Box 718
Flagstaff, AZ 86001
(928) 774-7488

International Mountain Biking Association
P.O. Box 7578
Boulder, CO 80306
(888) 442-IMBA
www.imba.com

Maine Island Trail Association
P.O. Box C
Rockland, Maine 04841
(207) 596-6456

National Outdoor Leadership School
Michael Cheek, LNT Program Coordinator
288 Main Street
Lander, WY 82520
(307) 335-2213
email: *michael_cheek@nols.edu*
www.nols.edu

National Park Service
Kelly Hartsell, LNT Coordinator
Shenandoah National Park, VA
(540) 999-3482
www.nps.gov

Scouting Ahead
c/o Washington Wilderness Coalition
4649 Sunnyside Avenue North
Seattle, WA 98105
(206) 633-1992

U.S. Forest Service
Tonto National Forest (Mesa Ranger District)
Greg Hansen, LNT Office
Phoenix, AZ
(480) 610-3300
www.fs.fed.us

Taking in the spectacular view from Yuma Point, Grand Canyon National Park
(Photo by Elias Butler)

Recommended Reading

Abbey, Edward. *Desert Solitaire*. New York: Ballantine Books, 1968.

Cole, David, and William Hammitt. *Wildland Recreation: Ecology and Management*. New York: John Wiley & Sons, 1987.

Cole, David, and Bruce Hampton. *Soft Paths*. Mechanicsburg, Penn.: NOLS/Stackpole Books, 1995.

Foreman, Dave, and Howie Wolke. *The Big Outside: A Descriptive Inventory of Big Wilderness Areas in the United States*. New York: Harmony Books, 1992.

Leave No Trace. "Alaskan Tundra." "Caving." "Desert and Canyons." "Horse Use." "Lakes Region." "Mountain Biking." "North America." "Northeast Mountains." "North Americas." "Pacific Northwest." "Rock Climbing." "Rocky Mountains." "Sea Kayaking." "Sierra Nevada." "Southeast." "Tropical Rainforests." "Western River Corridors." LNT Skills and Ethics Series, April 2001.

Leopold, Aldo. *A Sand County Almanac*. New York: Ballantine Books, 1970.

Meyer, Kathleen. *How to Shit in the Woods*. Berkeley, Calif.: Ten Speed Press, 1994.

Nash, Roderick. *Wilderness and the American Mind*. New Haven, Conn.: Yale University Press, 1982.

Wilson, Edward O. *The Future of Life*. Boston, Mass: Knopf, 2002.

Ancestral Puebloan petroglyphs in New Mexico *(Photo by Mike Frick)*

References

Introduction

Alt, Tom. Telephone conversation with author, August 1996.

Brame, Susan Chadwick, and Chad Henderson. *An Introduction to Wildland Ethics and Management*, 79. Lander, Wyo.: National Outdoor Leadership School, 1992.

Cole, David. "The Changing Wilderness." *Master Network* newsletter no. 8 (fall 1994).

———.Telephone conversation with author, July 1996.

———. Telephone interview with author, October 2002.

———. "Wilderness Recreation in the United States: Trends in Use, Users, and Impacts." *International Journal of Wilderness* 2, no. 3 (December 1996).

———. *Wilderness Recreation Use Trends, 1965 Through 1994*. U.S. Department of Agriculture Intermountain Research Station, April 1996. Available through *www.fs.fed.us/rm/main/pubs/notsohot_INT/rec_INT.html*.

Cole, David, and Beth Ranz. "Temporary Campsite Closures in the Selway–Bitterroot Wilderness." *Journal of Forestry* 81, no. 11 (November 1983): 729–32.

Hansen, Greg. Telephone interview with author, November 2002.

Marion, Jeff, and Scott Reid. *Development of the U.S. Leave No Trace Program: A Historical Perspective*. Blacksburg, Va.: National Park Service, Cooperative Park Studies Unit, Virginia Tech, January 2000.

Nash, Roderick. *Wilderness and the American Mind*. New Haven, Conn.: Yale University Press, 1982.

National Outdoor Leadership School. "Low-Impact Use of Arid Land Environments: A Bureau of Land Management Training Opportunity." Presented by NOLS at Clover Mountains Wilderness Study Area, March 1995: 57.

National Park System. *National Park System Visitation Report*, November 2002, NPS Visitation Database. *www.nps.gov/npstats*.

Spencer, Edward L., Herbert E. Echelberger, Raymond E. Leonard, and Craig Evans. "Trends in Hiking and Backcountry Use." In *Proceedings 1980 National Outdoor Recreation Trends Symposium.* Edited by Wilbur F. LaPage. U.S. Department of Agriculture, Forest Service, Northeast Forest Experiment Station, 1980: 195–98.

Thompson, Bill. Telephone conversation with author, October 1996.

U.S. Forest Service. *Proceedings of the Second Symposium on Social Aspects and Recreation Research, Pacific Southwest Research Station,* February 23–25, 1994.

U.S. Statutes at Large. 1964. Title 16, Chapter 23, Wilderness Act of 1964. Available at *http://lcweb2.loc.gov/ammem/amlaw/lwsl.html.*

Watts, Dana. Telephone interview and email exchange with author, November 2002.

Wyant, William K. *Westward in Eden: The Public Lands and the Conservation Movement,* 12–13. Berkeley, Calif.: University of California Press, 1978.

Chapter 1

Leave No Trace. "North America," Skills and Ethics series. April 2001.

National Outdoor Leadership School. Leave No Trace Master Educator Course Handbook.

Chapter 2

Cole, David. "Backcountry Impact Management: Lessons from Research." *Backcountry Recreation Management Trends* 31, no. 3 (1994): 10–14.

———. "Campsites in Three Western Wildernesses: Proliferation and Changes in Condition Over 12 to 16 Years." Ogden, Utah: U.S. Department of Agriculture, Forest Service, Intermountain Research Station, 1993.

———. "Monitoring the Conditions of Wilderness Campsites." Ogden, Utah: U.S. Department of Agriculture, Forest Service, Intermountain Research Station, 1983.

Cole, David, and William Hammitt. *Wildland Recreation: Ecology and Management.* New York: John Wiley & Sons, 1987.

Cole, David, Douglas McEwen, and Mark Simon. *Campsite Impacts in Four Wildernesses in the South-Central United States.* U.S. Department of Agriculture, Intermountain Research Station, July 1996.

Hart, John. *Walking Softly in the Wilderness.* San Francisco, Calif.: Sierra Club Books, 1984.

Marion, Jeff. *Camping Impact Management on the Appalachian National Scenic Trail.* Appalachian Trail Conference, Harpers Ferry, WV. April 2002.

———. *Results from the Application of a Campsite Inventory and Impact Monitoring System in Eleven Wilderness Areas of the Jefferson National Forest.*

Blacksburg, Va.: National Park Service, Cooperative Park Studies Unit, Virginia Tech, 1991.

Marion, Jeff, David Cole, and David Reynolds. "Limits of Acceptable Change: A Framework for Assessing Carrying Capacity." *Park Science*. Fall 1985: 9–10.

Marion, Jeff, Joseph Roggenbuck, and Robert Manning. *Problems and Practices in Backcountry Recreation Management: A Survey of National Park Service Managers*. Blacksburg, Va.: National Park Service, Cooperative Park Studies Unit, Virginia Tech, 1993.

Marion, Jeff, and Peter Williams. *Assessing Campsite Conditions for Limits of Acceptable Change Management in Shenandoah National Park*. Blacksburg, Va.: National Park Service, Cooperative Park Studies Unit, Virginia Tech, November 1995.

McGivney, Annette. "Stern Measures." *Backpacker*, October 1999: 50–56.

Monz, Chris. Interview with author, Lander, Wyoming, October 1996.

Smith, Del. Interview with author, November 1996.

Chapter 3

Brame, Rich. Interview with author, October 1996.

Cairncross, S. "Control of Enteric Pathogens in Developing Countries." In *Environmental Microbiology*, edited by R. Mitchell. New York: Wiley-Liss, Inc.; Washington, D.C.: World Health Organization, Regional Office for the Americas, 1992: 157–189.

Holmes, Daniel. *Experiments on the Effects of Human Urine and Trampling on Subalpine Plants*, 79. Berkeley, Calif.: University of California, Department of Geography, 1979.

Kimmel, Nadia. Telephone interview with author, October 2002.

Leemon, Dree. Correspondence with author, April 1997.

McGivney, Annette. "What's That Smell?" *Backpacker*, November 2000: 52–58.

Meyer, Kathleen. *How to Shit in the Woods*. Berkeley, Calif.: Ten Speed Press, 1994.

Monz, Chris. Interview with author, Lander, Wyoming, October 1996.

National Park Service Organic Act of 1916. U.S. Code. Vol. 43, secs. 1–410 (March 2, 1917).

Reeves, Harry. "Human Waste Disposal in the Sierran Wilderness." In *A Report on the Wilderness Impact Study*, 140. San Francisco: Sierra Club, 1979.

Sawyer, Marit. Correspondence with author, April 1997.

Temple, Kenneth L., Anne K. Camper, and Robert C. Lucas. "Potential Health Hazard from Human Wastes in Wilderness." *Journal of Soil and Water Conservation* 37, no. 6 (November–December 1982): 357–59.

Tilton, Buck. "Talking Dirty." *Backpacker*, May 1994: 48–53.

Chapter 4

Brockman, Frank, and Lawrence Merriam Jr. *Recreational Use of Wild Lands.* New York: McGraw-Hill Book Company, 1979.

Cole, David, and Richard Knight. "Effects of Recreational Activity on Wildlife in Wildlands." Trans. 56th N.A., Wildlands and National Resources Conference, 1991.

Cole, David, Joseph Roggenbuck, and Alan Watson. "Trends in Wilderness Recreation Use Characteristics." *Proceedings of the Fourth International Outdoor Recreation and Tourism Symposium.* University of Minnesota, May 1995.

Hammitt, William, and William Rutlin. "Use Encounter Standards and Curves for Achieved Privacy in Wilderness." *Leisure Sciences* 17, no. 4 (1995).

Jalbert, Linda. Telephone interview with author, November 2002.

Lee, Marty. Interview with author, October 2002.

Manning, Robert. *Studies in Outdoor Recreation: Search and Research for Satisfaction,* 2d ed. Corvallis, Ore.: Oregon State University Press, 1999.

Marion, Jeff, and Yu-Fai Leung. *Recreation Impacts and Management in Wilderness: A State-of-Knowledge Review.* USDA Forest Service Proceedings, Rocky Mountain Research Station 5 (2000).

Sharpe, Grant, Charles Odegaard, and Wenonah Finch Sharpe. *Park Management.* New York: John Wiley and Sons, 1983.

Chapters 5, 6, and 7

Blumenthal, Tim. Telephone conversation with author, November 1996.

Bricler, S., B. Tunnicliff, and J. Utter. "Use and Quality of Wildland Water: The Case of the Colorado River Corridor in the Grand Canyon." *Western Wildlands* 9 (1983): 20–25.

Cole, David. *Experimental Evaluations of Two Leave-No-Trace Techniques: Removing Boots and Using Geotextile Groundcloths.* U.S. Department of Agriculture Intermountain Research Station, November 1997.

Cole, David, and Mitchell McClaran. *Packstock in Wilderness: Use Impacts, Monitoring, and Management,* 3. Ogden, Utah: U.S. Department of Agriculture, Forest Service, Intermountain Research Station, 1993.

Crumbo, Kim. Telephone conversation with author, December 1996.

Leave No Trace. "Horse Use," Skills and Ethics series. April 2001.

———. "Mountain Biking," Skills and Ethics series. April 2001.

———. "Rock Climbing," Skills and Ethics series. April 2001.

———. "Western River Corridors," Skills and Ethics series. April 2001.

Magnuson, Mark. "Grand Teton National Park Sees Changes in Climbing." *Master Network* newsletter 9 (winter 1995).

Marion, Jeff. *An Assessment of Trail Conditions in Great Smoky Mountains National Park*, 127. Blacksburg, Va.: U.S. Department of Interior, National Park Service, Southeast Region, 1993.

———. Correspondence with author, October 2002.

———. "Trekking Poles: Can You Save Your Knees and the Environment?" *The Register* 24, no. 5 (spring 2001).

Matous, Steve. Telephone conversation with author, March 2003.

Mink, Virgil. Telephone conversation with author, September 1997.

National Sporting Goods Association. *The Sporting Goods Market in 1996*. Orlando, Fla.: National Sporting Goods Association, 1995.

Olson-Rutz, K. M., C. B. Marlow, and K. Hansen. "Recovery of High Elevation Plant Community After Packhorse Grazing." *Journal of Range Management* 49, no. 6 (November 1996).

Outdoor Recreation Coalition of America. *State of the Industry Report*. Boulder, Colo.: Outdoor Recreation Coalition of America, 1995.

Quarrier, Sid. Telephone conversation with author, December 1996.

Walka, Pete. Telephone interview with author, November 2002.

Willard, B. E., and J. W. Marr. "Recovery of alpine tundra under protection after damage by human activities in the Rocky Mountains of Colorado." *Biological Conservation* 1, no. 31(1971): 181–90.

Wilson, John, and Joseph Seney. "Erosional Impact of Hikers, Horses, Motorcycles, and Off-Road Bicycles on Mountain Trails in Montana." *Mountain Research and Development* 14, no. 1 (1994): 77–88.

Chapter 8

Cole, David, and Bruce Hampton. *Soft Paths*. Mechanicsburg, Penn.: NOLS/Stackpole Books, 1995.

Cooper, D. J. "The Arrigetch Peaks Region of the Central Brooks Range, Alaska: Ecosystems and Human Use." *Proceedings of the National Wilderness Conference Current Research*. Ogden, Utah: USDA Forest Service General Technical Report, Intermountain Research Station, 1985: 94–99.

Foti, Pam. Interview with author, October 2002.

Ganci, Dave. *Desert Hiking*. Berkeley, Calif.: Wilderness Press, 1993.

Leave No Trace. "Deserts and Canyons," Skills and Ethics series. April 2001.

Library of Congress. Statutes at Large. Available online at *http://lcweb2.loc.gov/ammem/amlaw/lwsl.html.*

Miller, Debbie S. *Midnight Wilderness: Journeys in Alaska's Arctic National Wildlife Refuge*. San Francisco: Sierra Club Books, 1990.

Moore, Rick. *Preserving Traces of the Past: Protecting the Colorado Plateau's Archaeological Heritage*. Flagstaff, Ariz.: The Grand Canyon Trust, 1994.

Chapter 9

Bates, Dave. Correspondence with author, October 2002.

Boy Scouts of America. *The Boy Scout Handbook: Trail to Eagle*. Irving, Tex.: Boy Scouts of America, 1998.

Daniels, Scott. "Leave No Trace." *Scouting*, March/April 1999.

Gookin, John. "Empowering Children with Active Learning Techniques." *Master Network* newsletter 6 (winter 1994).

Hall, Adrienne. Telephone conversation with author, August 1997.

Hansen, Greg. Telephone conversation with author, August 1997.

Leave No Trace, Inc. *Teaching Leave No Trace: Activities for Teaching Responsible Outdoor Skills*. Boulder, Colo.: Leave No Trace, Inc., 1996.

Leopold, Aldo. *A Sand County Almanac*. New York: Ballantine Books, 1970.

Munoz, James. Correspondence with author, November 2002.

Sawyer, Marit, ed. *Scouting Ahead*, 3d ed. Seattle: Washington Wilderness Coalition, 1996.

USDA Forest Service. *The Wilderness Ranger Training Manual*. Helena, Mont.: Arthur Carhart National Wilderness Training Center, 1995.

Index

About the Author

As Southwest Editor for *Backpacker* magazine, Annette McGivney makes her living in America's great outdoors. In addition to writing about her adventures in the deserts and mountains of the Southwest, McGivney specializes in environmental topics and personality profiles. While on assignment for *Backpacker*, she's hiked with all types of offbeat wilderness enthusiasts—from survivalists to psychics to rattlesnake researchers. McGivney's proximity to the Grand Canyon and other large Southwest wilderness areas puts her in the middle of the West's most controversial public lands debates.

McGivney is also a part-time faculty member of Northern Arizona University's School of Communication, where she teaches journalism and outdoor writing courses.

McGivney's six-year-old son Austin and husband Mike join her on many backpacking trips. The family's favorite place to hike is the San Francisco Peaks Wilderness near Flagstaff, Arizona.

THE MOUNTAINEERS, founded in 1906, is a nonprofit outdoor activity and conservation club, whose mission is "to explore, study, preserve, and enjoy the natural beauty of the outdoors . . . . " Based in Seattle, Washington, the club is now the third-largest such organization in the United States, with seven branches throughout Washington State.

The Mountaineers sponsors both classes and year-round outdoor activities in the Pacific Northwest, which include hiking, mountain climbing, ski-touring, snowshoeing, bicycling, camping, kayaking and canoeing, nature study, sailing, and adventure travel. The club's conservation division supports environmental causes through educational activities, sponsoring legislation, and presenting informational programs. All club activities are led by skilled, experienced volunteers, who are dedicated to promoting safe and responsible enjoyment and preservation of the outdoors.

If you would like to participate in these organized outdoor activities or the club's programs, consider a membership in The Mountaineers. For information and an application, write or call The Mountaineers, Club Headquarters, 300 Third Avenue West, Seattle, WA 98119; 206-284-6310.

The Mountaineers Books, an active, nonprofit publishing program of the club, produces guidebooks, instructional texts, historical works, natural history guides, and works on environmental conservation. All books produced by The Mountaineers Books fulfill the club's mission.

Send or call for our catalog of more than 500 outdoor titles:

The Mountaineers Books
1001 SW Klickitat Way, Suite 201
Seattle, WA 98134
800-553-4453
mbooks@mountaineersbooks.org
www.mountaineersbooks.org

The Mountaineers Books is proud to be a corporate sponsor of Leave No Trace, whose mission is to promote and inspire responsible outdoor recreation through education, research, and partnerships. The Leave No Trace program is focused specifically on human-powered (nonmotorized) recreation.

Leave No Trace strives to educate visitors about the nature of their recreational impacts, as well as offer techniques to prevent and minimize such impacts. Leave No Trace is best understood as an educational and ethical program, not as a set of rules and regulations.

For more information, visit *www.LNT.org,* or call 800-332-4100.

MORE TITLES IN THE BACKPACKER MAGAZINE SERIES FROM THE MOUNTAINEERS BOOKS:

TENT AND CAR CAMPER'S HANDBOOK: Advice for Families & First-Timers
Buck Tilton & Kristin Hostetter
The Lowdown on family car camping and tent camping—no experience necessary!

HIKING LIGHT HANDBOOK: Carry Less, Enjoy More
Karen Berger
Practical strategies for everyone who'd like to lighten their load on the trail.

TREKKER'S HANDBOOK: Strategies to Enhance Your Journey
Buck Tilton
Contains pre-trip, during the trip, and post-trip strategies for long-distance hiking.

WINTER HIKING AND CAMPING: Managing Cold for Comfort and Safety
Mike Lanza
Cold is your friend—embrace it. Hit the trail and camp even when the temps are down.

EVERYDAY WISDOM: 1001 Expert Tips for Hikers
Karen Berger
Expert tips and tricks for hikers and backpackers selected from one of the most popular Backpacker magazine columns.

MORE EVERYDAY WISDOM: Trail-Tested Advice from the Experts
Karen Berger
More tips for enhancing backcountry trips.

BACKCOUNTRY COOKING: From Pack to Plate in 10 Minutes
Dorcas Miller
Over 144 recipes and how to plan simple meals.

Available at fine bookstores and outdoor stores, by phone at 800-553-4453 or on the Web at *www.mountaineersbooks.org*

THE MOUNTAINEERS BOOKS